DECO BY THE BAY

100 Bush Street, Shell Building, designed by George Kelham, built in 1929; front entrance. Photograph by Douglas Keister, Oakland, California.

MICHAEL F. CROWE

DECO

BY THE

BAY

Art Deco
Architecture in the
San Francisco Bay Area

VIKING
STUDIO
BOOKS

This book is dedicated to my parents
Pearl and Tom Crowe
who lived during the period
and taught me all about it.

NOTE TO THE READER
Unless otherwise indicated,
the photographs in this book
are by the author.

VIKING STUDIO BOOKS
Published by the Penguin Group
Penguin Books USA Inc., 375 Hudson Street,
New York, New York, 10014, U.S.A.

Penguin Books Ltd, 27 Wrights Lane,
London W8 5TZ, England

Penguin Books Australia Ltd, Ringwood,
Victoria, Australia

Penguin Books Canada Ltd, 2801 John Street,
Markham, Ontario, Canada L3R 1B4

Penguin Books (N.Z.) Ltd, 182-90 Wairau Road,
Auckland 10, New Zealand

Penguin Books Ltd, Registered Offices:
Harmondsworth, Middlesex, England

First published by Viking Studio Books, an imprint of Penguin Books USA Inc.

First printing, February 1995
10 9 8 7 6 5 4 3 2 1

Copyright © Michael F. Crowe 1995
All rights reserved

Library of Congress Catalog Card Number: 94-60981

Book designed by Nancy Danahy
Printed and bound by Dai Nippon Printing Co., Hong Kong, Ltd.

ISBN: 0-525-48621-6 (paperback); 0-525-93856-7 (cloth)

CONTENTS

3008 Geary Boulevard,
Bridge Theater,
built in 1939.

THE ART DECO STYLE
AND ITS SOURCES

Lights! Camera! Action! Deco! Theatricality pervades the Art Deco style. What Deco building doesn't conjure up visions of sleek automobiles parked in front with fashionable, elegantly dressed people emerging and ambling gracefully into the well-appointed lobby? But these associations with glamour and modernity, fully realized in movie houses of the twenties and thirties, are only part of the story. San Francisco, like every other American city, has its share of these Art Deco buildings.

Entered from the east across the Oakland-San Francisco Bay Bridge, or from the north across the Golden Gate Bridge, the Art Deco-inspired bridges set the stage for the city's Art Deco glories. While the Deco buildings of San Francisco don't have a particular regional stamp like the tropical touches in Miami Beach or Indian motifs in the Southwest, they are some of the finest examples of Deco to be found anywhere in the state of California. All of these buildings and buildings like them around the world share a common design inspiration, a desire by the architects to create buildings in a modern style. But why is there this commonality and where did it come from?

Art Deco is a twentieth-century design movement, but it is not a phenomenon unique to America. What we know as Art Deco resulted from an exposition held in Paris in 1925, entitled *L'Exposition Internationale des Arts Décoratifs and Industriels Modernes*. This event, held from April to October, was the culmination of a variety of forces: art movements, intellectual ideas, and an expanding technology, not to mention the persistence of the French design community. The organizers, led by the *Société des Artistes Décorateurs*, intended to showcase the new designs being produced in Europe. Hence the name "Moderne" and the strict entry rules that required exhibitors to have buildings and wares that presented only the most currently styled items, and which were not based on any historic period of design or art.

France was the host country, and in the largest exhibit areas it displayed modern items along with the other participating nations. Most of the European countries were represented, including the post-World War I-established countries of Poland and Czechoslovakia. Germany, the archenemy of France in the war, was pointedly not invited. The United States was not represented because the invitation had been declined by the U.S. government, which begged off with the observation that there was no modern art in America and

1. 1750 Vallejo Street, apartment building; detail of stucco on the façade.

4. 4769-3 Mission Street, Royal Baking Co., built in 1932; detail of ornament on the façade.

5. 742 Grant Avenue, commercial building; detail of ornament on the façade.

2. 1130 Howard Street, industrial building; detail of the entry.

3. 99 Ord Street, house, built in 1932; detail of the entry.

American designers were not designing in a modern style.

The buildings, temporarily constructed for the Exposition and designed by the leading European architects, provided the sources for the architectural and decorative designs that would be used in San Francisco and throughout the world for the next two decades. These motifs provided the grist for the designers who produced public buildings, schools, apartments, interiors, furniture, textiles, and fashions soon after the event.

Art Deco ornament (figs. 1–18) is characterized by zigzags, chevrons, rays, stepped arches, stylized floral and natural forms, and simplified and overlapping forms. They can be found in all areas of design from skyscrapers to toasters. The origins for these forms lie in the developments in the art world in Germany and France in the years before World War I. Undoubtedly, Cubism, with its emphasis on geometric elements, was a major influence in the stylization of floral forms and ultimately other ornamental forms derived from classical sources such as columns, fluting, and floral ornament.

The use of zigzags, chevrons, and rays can be found in German Expressionist graphics and on some early German buildings from the turn of the century. A few Czech architects briefly flirted with Cubist designs in architecture at about the same time. The new designs were enhanced by an approach to color combining stark contrasts in both color and intensity that were derived from the art movements of Fauvism and Cubism, the costumes and sets of the Ballets Russes, and African textiles. The Fauvists explored the use of color through its contrast and placement. Cubism in its early stages used a palette of gray, yellow, black, cream, and green that subsequently came to be used in a range of items from wallpapers to carpets. The forms and colors of African textiles provided a completely new source for design not tied to the classical tradition of western Europe and offering a change that was new and exciting.

Some of these design ideas had been published in the United States prior to the 1925 Exposition; also, American architects had served in World War I or had flocked to Europe after the end of the

6. 100 Bush Street, Shell Building, designed by George Kelham, built in 1929; detail of plaster ornament over the elevator doors.

7. 75 Buena Vista East, apartment building, designed by Albert Larsen, built in 1930; detail of molded ornament over the entry arch.

8. 640 Mason Street, apartment building, designed by Herman C. Baumann, built in 1932; detail of molded ornament in the entry.

9. 1930 Steiner Street, designed by E. V. Cobby, built in 1931; detail of molded ornament in entry.

10. 1050 Franklin Street, apartment building; detail of molded-stucco ornament on the façade.

11. 2425 Buchanan Street, apartment building, built in 1931; detail of molded-plaster spandrel ornament.

war. Earlier, the famous 1913 Armory Show in New York City had provoked a stir in the American art world by showing the works of Picasso, Modigliani, Matisse, Duchamp, and Brancusi, among others. In some American cities, French perfumers had remodeled their shops and presented their scents in bottles reflecting the latest European styles. The Wiener Werkstätte, an avant-garde design movement located in Vienna, briefly had an outlet in New York City. But despite these modernist developments American designers remained conservative and continued to produce revivalist versions of French- and English-inspired designs. "Louis whatever" furniture graced the interiors of chateauesque or medieval manor houses, or, particularly in California, Spanish Colonial Revival villas.

It was the Paris Exposition that brought all of the modernist design forces together in one place and provided the opportunity for artists and designers from all over the world to see and learn from each other. The United States sent a delegation of architects, artists, and designers to the event with the express purpose of learning what was current in the world of design. And they did just that. Upon the return of the delegation museums and department stores presented displays of the art, clothing, furniture, and decorations. Interiors magazines, advertising copy and illustrations, and industry catalogs published in the years immediately following the Exposition show that the modernist influence was slowly beginning to be adopted by American industry.

But it was the movies that introduced modern design to the general American public, as early as 1926. Glamorously clad stars walked and danced through settings displaying the latest in furniture, lighting fixtures, and decoration. Americans from the largest city to the smallest town that had a movie theater quickly learned what modern design could mean in their lives—certainly not at Hollywood's scale of interpretation, but more reasonably in the local five-and-dime incarnations of the style.

In addition to the European forces, there were other currents that contributed to

12. 4150 Clement Street, Veterans Administration Hospital, built in 1934; detail of molded terra-cotta spandrel ornament.

13. 3665 Scott Street, apartment building, designed by Irvine and Ebbetts, built in 1933; detail of molded entry ornament.

the designs of the period, once they had caught on in America. In architecture, the New York zoning laws requiring buildings to have setbacks became accepted practice, if not law, in many parts of the country. The Russ Building (fig. 19) by George Kelham in downtown San Francisco is a prime example of this stepped-back look in highrises. While the profile rises in stages, its Gothic Revival detailing is a typical, if conservative, adaptation of two different design sources. In addition, the American design world was beginning to feel the impact of the arrival of such designers as Raymond Loewy, Norman Bel Geddes, and Donald Deskey.

Raymond Loewy is best known for introducing the principles of streamlining through his design work, particularly for the Pennsylvania Railroad, his automobile designs for the Hupmobile, and for Sears & Roebuck's Coldspot refrigerators. All his designs reflect the rounding of forms, suppression of protruding elements, and an emphasis on smooth, sleek finishes. These streamlining elements and the use of "speed whiskers or speed lines" (three parallel lines) came into full form in the thirties.

14. 1695 Beach Street, apartment building, built in 1931; detail of entry with stepped arch and molded-plaster ornament.

15. *1600 Beach Street, apartment building, built in 1936; detail of molded ornament and black-glass strips over ornament.*

16. *1150 Union Street, apartment building, designed by Albert Larsen, built in 1930; molded-plaster ornament in spandrels and around garage entry.*

17. *1299 Jones Street, Clay-Jones Apartments, designed by Albert Larsen, built in 1930; detail of molded ornament in entry.*

Norman Bel Geddes is most often recognized for his futuristic designs for ships and airplanes bearing the streamlined look, but he also produced numerous designs for both commercial and domestic interiors. Donald Deskey showed the influence of his European travel and study in his use of industrial materials, such as chrome, aluminum, and steel, in his designs for interiors, furniture, and housewares produced by the firm of Deskey-Vollmer.

American designers further combined European designs with other influences, such as Mayan architecture from Mexico and Central America, to create designs that are now recognized as Art Deco. The use of Mayan-style ornament is not surprising. The architecture of the Mayans incorporated stepped arches, flattened and stylized floral and animal forms, and a somewhat Cubist look that fit into the emerging Art Deco design vocabulary. It is not unusual then to find American architects looking to such a source from this hemisphere, much as the European designers looked to Egypt and the Middle East for their design

18. 23rd Street and Ocean; house; Cubist massing of forms.

19. 235 Montgomery Street, Russ Building, designed by George Kelham, built in 1927; stepped profile of massing.

sources. It was all a part of finding inspiration in alternatives to the classical architectural heritage and design vocabulary of Greece and Rome, which designers then viewed as a burden in expressing modernity.

Technology also became an important element in the development of the style. Aluminum, more readily available because of the abundant supply of electricity needed in its refining, was used in many new ways, both structural and decorative. Other products developed earlier in the century, such as Bakelite, were exploited through creative uses from appliances to jewelry. New products were invented like Formica, which offered ways of producing surfaces with the sleek, clean lines that proclaimed modernity for both the material and the item.

During the period there were further changes in the way ornament was used. In the late twenties architectural ornament tended to be used more profusely, especially around the entry door and in the window spandrels as on the apartment building at 1150 Union Street, designed by Albert Larsen (fig. 20). By about 1933–1935, ornament began to be less prominent in these locations. Often the ornament was simplified to become only incised lines or reeding in the spandrels: the apartment building at 3560 19th Street (fig. 21) is a good example of this later phase. What late in the

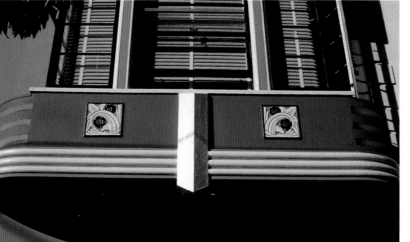

1920s had been elaborately molded friezes of floral ornament, by the mid-1930s often became simple pulvinated or raised speed lines. Floral ornament was often limited to roundels or octagonal plaques (fig. 22).

Glass block became popular by the early thirties and was used in all kinds of arrangements, in simple bands or as stepped inserts like those found on either side of the entrance to the apartment building at 1700 Bay Street (see fig. 117), or the dramatic glass-brick elevator shaft at the façade of the apartment building at 1360 Montgomery Street (fig. 23). The building at 3060 Scott Street, designed by Herman C. Baumann, has glass block at the entry walls and as a surround for the entry door (fig. 24). It was also used for interior walls, with the broadcasting building at 420 Taylor Street being one of the best examples.

Pigmented glass, sometimes called carrera glass, or by various

20. 1150 Union Street, apartment building, designed by Albert Larsen, built in 1930; has molded-plaster ornament in spandrels and around entry.

21. 3560 19th Street, apartment building, built in 1941; molded-plaster speed lines and floral plaques.

22. 375 Guerrero Street, flats building, built in 1936; molded-plaster plaques.

23. 1360 Montgomery Street, apartment building, designed by S. W. Goldstein, built in 1936; front entrance. Photograph by Douglas Keister, Oakland, California.

24. 3060 Scott Street, apartment building, designed by Herman C. Baumann, built in 1937; glass-block entry surround.

25. 1900 Beach Street, apartment building, designed by Herman C. Baumann, built in 1936; detail of entry with strips of black sand-blasted glass.

trade names such as Vitrolux, was also used on façades. It came in many different colors that were often used on storefronts. Residential use was often limited to simple black strips, or it was also sandblasted with floral designs as panels near the entry. This kind of treatment can be seen on the buildings at 3060 Scott Street (fig. 24) and 1900 Beach Street (fig. 25).

Architects combined these forces of design and technology in the twenties and thirties to produce the modern style that we now call Art Deco in reference to the Paris Exposition of 1925 that provided the showcase and inspiration. During the period the style was known as the Moderne or modernistic style. In any case, the architects in San Francisco accepted it, developed it, and left a legacy of structures that invite our appreciation and enjoyment.

ART DECO ARCHITECTURE
IN SAN FRANCISCO

The first large-scale building in San Francisco to show the impact of the new European influences was the Pacific Telephone Company Building designed by Timothy Pflueger and constructed in 1926 (fig. 26). The stepped massing of the building owes a debt to the design by Eliel Saarinen for the Chicago Tribune architectural competition. In the Saarinen design the building elevation is stepped back at the seventeenth, nineteenth, twenty-second, and twenty-fourth floors. The Pflueger building also moves up in stages, stepping back at the upper floors. While the details of the ornament on the Saarinen design are not readily evident in the published drawings, the Pflueger building is enriched with decorated cornices at each of the setback floors. A small but noticeable detail in both designs is a series of round-arched windows at the top floor of each setback (fig. 27).

The exterior of the Pflueger building is gray terra-cotta with inventive ornament over the entire façade. The entrance tympanum hints at the decorative scheme of the lobby. Just above the entry is what can best be described as "flying phone books" or winged books (fig. 28). The top of the building is crowned with both stylized flowers and eagles, the symbol of communication. On the lower levels of the setbacks are stylized bluebells, the flower of the telephone company. All of the ornament gives a rich plasticity to the building.

The entry lobby, which has been recently restored, is stunning. It has the basic design elements that Pflueger would repeat in his other influential buildings: dark marble walls setting off an elaborate plaster ceiling showing classic influences from the period (figs. 29, 30). Here, the ceiling simulates a piece of Chinese brocade or lacquerwork highlighted by pierced lantern-like light fixtures.

Pflueger followed this work in 1928 with his 450 Sutter Building (figs. 31, 32), constructed as a medical-arts building. It was one of the first Mayan Revival-style buildings in the city. The exterior is pale beige terra cotta set in a zigzag plan with incised Mayan-style ornament (fig. 33). In the lobby the dark marble walls set off an elaborately detailed stepped-arch ceiling with ornament derived from Mayan architecture (fig. 34). The tympanum ornament and the molded ornament around the entry carry out the Mayan motifs further.

The 450 Sutter Building was regarded as unusual for the city when it was first built because it contained a garage integrated into the building and had a novel plan with canted bays. The plan was enhanced by the special cladding method for the terra cotta (see fig. 34) that allowed it to be attached by wires rather than the usual metal armature. Thus the walls were thinner and the superstructure lighter, all mak-

26. *140 New Montgomery Street, Pacific Telephone Company Building, designed by Timothy Pflueger for Miller & Pflueger, built in 1926; stepped profile.*

27. *140 New Montgomery Street, Pacific Telephone Company Building, designed by Timothy Pflueger for Miller & Pflueger, built in 1926; detail of stepped profile.*

28. *140 New Montgomery Street, Pacific Telephone Company Building, designed by Timothy Pflueger for Miller & Pflueger, built in 1926; detail of ornament over entry.*

29. 140 New Montgomery Street,
Pacific Telephone Company Building,
designed by Timothy Pflueger for
Miller & Pflueger, built in 1926;
entry lobby. Photograph by Douglas
Keister, Oakland, California.

30. *140 New Montgomery Street, Pacific Telephone Company Building, designed by Timothy Pflueger for Miller & Pflueger, built in 1926; detail of the ceiling in the entry lobby. Photograph by Douglas Keister, Oakland, California.*

31. *450 Sutter Street, medical-arts building, designed by Timothy Pflueger for Miller & Pflueger, built in 1928.*

32. *450 Sutter Street, medical-arts building, designed by Timothy Pflueger for Miller & Pflueger, built in 1928; detail of façade showing entry canopy.*

33. *450 Sutter Street, medical-arts building, designed by Timothy Pflueger for Miller & Pflueger, built in 1928; detail showing Mayan-inspired ornament on the façade.*

34. 450 Sutter Street, medical-arts building, designed by Timothy Pflueger for Miller & Pflueger, built in 1928; entry lobby. Photograph by Douglas Keister, Oakland, California.

35. 155 Sansome Street, Stock Exchange Building, designed by Timothy Pflueger for Miller & Pflueger, built in 1929; detail of building entry.

36. 155 Sansome Street, Stock Exchange Building, designed by Timothy Pflueger for Miller & Pflueger, built in 1929; building lobby.

ing the construction more economical and with more rentable space per square foot on each floor.

But it was Pflueger's Stock Exchange Building of 1929 at 155 Sansome Street (fig. 35) that had an even more direct influence in the city, notably in the apartment buildings on Nob Hill, and in the Pacific Heights and Marina districts of the city. For the Stock Exchange Building lobby Pflueger again used his formula of dark marble walls to set off an ornate molded-plaster ceiling. While there may be a passing resemblance to a gilded waffle iron (figs. 36, 37), or perhaps to Persian star-motif tiles, the designer, Michael Goodman, explained the source differently.

Goodman had visited a German Expressionist nightclub in Berlin and was taken with the faceted and mirrored ceiling. This appeared to be just what he wanted for the entrance lobby at the Stock Exchange Building. However, the city building department thought otherwise, probably for seismic concerns, and Goodman settled for gilding the molded plaster surface. Once more these elements coalesced to create a rich effect. It is the molded-plaster ceiling that was imitated by other architects to enliven the lobbies of numerous apartment buildings.

The upper two floors of the building comprise what is now known as the City Club. It has an outstanding interior highlighted by a Diego Rivera mural on the staircase, his first in this country. The themes in the mural of electricity, industry, commerce, and agriculture illustrate the "golds" of California. These themes of industry and leisure activity were further carried out by other artists in bas-reliefs, and in the painted and sandblasted glass found throughout the interior, which still retains much

37. *155 Sansome Street, Stock Exchange Building, designed by Timothy Pflueger for Miller & Pflueger, built in 1929; detail of lobby ceiling.*

38. *155 Sansome Street, Stock Exchange Building, built in 1929; overmantel decoration in City Club designed by Michael Goodman. Photograph by Douglas Keister, Oakland, California.*

39. *155 Sansome Street, Stock Exchange Building, built in 1929; elevator doors in City Club designed by Michael Goodman. Photograph by Douglas Keister, Oakland, California.*

40. 600 32nd Avenue, George Washington High School, designed by Timothy Pflueger for Miller & Pflueger, built in 1930; main façade.

of its original furniture. The club has recently undergone a refurbishing that has preserved the original elements (figs. 38, 39).

Pflueger's George Washington High School (fig. 40), constructed just a few years later, shows the beginnings of streamlining as it was interpreted in the city. It appears symmetrical at first glance, but the south wing with its curved details and glass blocks shows the elements that would characterize this later phase of Art Deco.

Pflueger theaters still remain throughout the city and the state. His Castro Theater, one of his earliest, is unmistakably Spanish Colonial Revival in style but the marquee and vertical sign give it a Deco touch (fig. 41), the result of the work of Alexander Aimwell Cantin in 1935. The Paramount Theater in Oakland is Pflueger's crowning achievement in theater design (fig. 42). The façade is most unusual with its portrayal of towering figures manipulating marionettes. It draws its inspiration from one of the entrance gates to the 1925 Paris Exposition, where giant figures were also used.

The interior of the theater has a stunning two-story lobby with a suspended ceiling of back-lit, molded, galvanized sheet metal, which is also used in the theater auditorium (figs. 43, 44). Pflueger had first used this material in his remodeling of the Pacific Coast Stock Exchange trading room. He called the metal elements "fins" and used them again in the Black Patent Leather lounge in the St. Francis Hotel, which no longer exists.

Pflueger's Royal Theater on Polk Street in San Francisco still has the upper portions of the façade intact, although it has been painted (fig. 45). Further north on Polk Street is his Alhambra Theater designed in a Moorish style with some Deco touches that have been recently refurbished on the interior (fig. 46). Like the Castro Theater, both of these theaters have signs and marquees designed by Cantin. Cantin was an associate of Pflueger's for the Pacific Telephone

41. 429 Castro Street, Castro Theater, designed by Timothy Pflueger for Miller & Pflueger, built in 1922; main façade.

42. *2025 Broadway, Oakland, Paramount Theater, designed by Timothy Pflueger for Miller & Pflueger, built in 1931; main façade.*

43. *2025 Broadway, Oakland, Paramount Theater, designed by Timothy Pflueger for Miller & Pflueger, built in 1931; the lobby. Photograph by Douglas Keister, Oakland, California.*

44. 2025 Broadway, Oakland, Paramount Theater, designed by Timothy Pflueger for Miller & Pflueger, built in 1931; the auditorium. Photograph by Douglas Keister, Oakland, California.

Building and designed numerous theaters on the West Coast. His Orinda Theater in Orinda, California, was recently restored.

Pflueger's other notable theater in the Bay Area is in Alameda, across the bay from the city (see figs. 136, 137). It was built at the same time as the Paramount, and although it was almost as large in seating capacity, it was not as large in terms of lobby areas. It has recently fallen on hard times, and despite the removal of all of the seats, a great deal of the decorative elements still remain, including some of the light fixtures and portions of the carpet with the "martini-olive" design.

While Timothy Pflueger left his imprint on the city and the state with a rich legacy of highrise and institutional buildings, including the Oakland–San Francisco Bay Bridge, other architects made important contributions to the Art Deco architectural heritage of the city. George Kelham, a Beaux Arts-trained architect, was already well known when he designed the Shell Building (fig. 47) at the corner of Bush and Battery. He had originally come to San Francisco to supervise the construction of the Palace Hotel after the 1906 earthquake and fire, and he remained.

Kelham's Shell Building was hailed at the time for its original design. The exterior is terra cotta with a marble-like texture. The profile is stepped and was originally lit at night with amber floodlights. The built-in light pods are visible around the upper level of the cornice. Near the base, above the third floor, are stylized floral elements, which are very characteristic of the style. The interior lobby, recently altered to increase the height of the ceiling, still retains portions of the original

45. 1529 Polk Street, Royal
Theater, designed by Timothy
Pflueger for Miller & Pflueger;
main façade.

46. Polk Street, Alhambra
Theater, designed by Timothy
Pflueger for Miller and Pflueger,
built in 1928, with additional
work by Alex A. Cantin in 1935;
façade.

design, most notably the elevator doors with back-lit molded plaster rays surmounting the doors trimmed with lotus flowers. The lotus flowers are a lingering influence from the discovery in 1922 of King Tutankhamen's tomb in Egypt, which had set off a rage for decorative designs in the Egyptian style.

Kelham's other designs include the main Public Library in the Civic Center and the Russ Building. The library is unmistakably Classic Revival, while the Russ Building has Gothic detailing. His Marina Middle School (fig. 48) of 1936 shows the influence of streamlining. His work at the University of California at Berkeley, the Life Sciences Building (fig. 49), displays what can best be described as "Greco Deco" style, with stylized columns and other ornament derived from a classical vocabulary but given a modernistic stamp. He used the same style for the Memorial Stadium, also at Berkeley (fig. 50).

Kelham is typical of classically trained architects of the period who rapidly assimilated the elements of the Deco style into their repertoire. For this reason, the quality of the building ornament reflects the training the architects had received in drawing and producing ornament. Kelham is probably the best example of this phenomenon.

Another architect who left his stamp on the city is Herman C. Baumann. His specialty was domestic buildings, including highrise apartment buildings, smaller six-story apartments, three-story apartments-over-garage buildings, two-story flats buildings, and single-family residences. His career began in 1910, and his early buildings reflect the prevailing architectural styles. In the early twenties he was the master of the Spanish Colonial Revival style and Renaissance/Mediterranean style. Many of these buildings still can be found throughout the city, often facing one of his later Art Deco buildings. By 1931, he had designed more than five hundred such buildings. In the late twenties and early thirties, he assimilated the elements of Art Deco in the many buildings he designed, particularly in the Marina and Pacific Heights districts.

One of his earliest buildings incorporating Art Deco elements is the highrise apartment building at Green and Leavenworth, built in 1928. In overall massing it owes a great deal to Pflueger's Pacific Telephone Company Building at 120 New Montgomery Street, built in 1926. Baumann's Green Street Building has the same stepped massing and round arched windows on the top floor. In addition, the placement of the molded ornament at the cornice shows the further influence of the Pflueger design. Baumann used these details, in conjunction with unique molded ornament, to create his own vocabulary for decorating structures. The round arched windows can be found on the apartment building at 1870 Pacific (fig. 51); the unusual molded ornament at the cornice of the Telephone Company Building has its parallel in the "flowerpot" ornament at 1870 Pacific and 3060 Scott Street. While these designs are obvious simplifications of the more complex designs of Pflueger and Saarinen, they show the ability of a local architect to transfer the elements of high-style buildings into a popular local architectural vocabulary. Albert Larsen used these same design elements in his Clay-Jones Apartments at 1299 Jones Street. There is a small-scale domestic version of these highrise apartments at 815 Miramar (fig. 52). The house also has a stepped profile, albeit of only two stories, and the windows are round-arched like those in the highrises.

48. 3500 Fillmore Street, Marina Middle School, designed by George Kelham and Will P. Day, built in 1936; auditorium wing.

Much like the nineteenth-century San Francisco house builders who used characteristic signature touches on their houses, Baumann also had signature design elements that can be found on his building exteriors and interiors. Many of his buildings have three-sided bays with the underside of the bay finished off with decorative detailing. In some instances the edge is

47. 100 Bush Street, Shell Building, designed by George Kelham, built in 1929; main elevation.

25

50. *Berkeley Campus, University of California Memorial Stadium, designed by George Kelham; detail of stadium.*

49. *Berkeley Campus, University of California Life Sciences Building, designed by George Kelham; detail of end pavilion.*

51. *1870 Pacific Street, apartment building, designed by Herman C. Baumann, built in 1937; detail of cornice.*

merely scalloped as at 640 Mason Street, or has an underside with molded-plaster ornament as at 845 California Street or 55 Hermann Street (fig. 53). By the mid-thirties he had replaced this lush floral ornament with simple "prisms" that often begin in the window spandrels and continue to the underside of the bay.

Baumann's lobby interiors have wonderful decorative elements (fig. 54). Some of the buildings still retain their original plaster finishes and colors. He regularly used combed plaster walls, with molded plaster used at the cornice and in decorative mirrored panels set into the walls. In the larger buildings with two-story lobbies, his "signature" is to be seen in the upper wall that has an opening opposite the entry door. These lobbies can be found at 845 California, 55 Hermann Street, 1950 Clay (fig. 55), and 3401 Clay. Ceilings have either the "City Club Style," with a gilded molded design, or they have a more traditional coffered effect. Sometimes the coffered ceilings are combined with stenciled beams. Later in the thirties, Baumann dispensed with the molded ceilings and used a flat surface with stenciled designs, sometimes used with metallic paint as in the apartment building at 1700 Bay (fig. 56).

On the exterior, the entry is usually flanked with light sconces and a hanging light fixture over the door. The original fixtures remain at 55 Hermann Street, 843 California (fig. 57), and 3401 Clay Street, while at 640 Mason the original interior wall sconces are still in place.

Baumann also designed buildings in Oakland, Sacramento, and Burlingame. His most notable building in Oakland is the Bellevue Staten Apartments on the

52. 815 Miramar Street, house; main elevation.

53. 55 Hermann Street, Allen Arms Apartments, designed by Herman C. Baumann, built in 1931; detail of underside of bay windows.

shores of Lake Merritt (fig. 58). Its highrise Deco profile adds excitement to the view at the end of the lake.

The Bellevue Staten Apartments building was constructed in 1928 and is a good example of what could be termed "schizophrenic" Deco. The first several floors and the lobby interior are in the Spanish Colonial Revival style but the cornice, in buff-colored terra cotta, is a combination of fantasy shapes seemingly taken out of a Buck Rogers movie, but probably more influenced by Pflueger's ornament on the Pacific Telephone Company Building. The apartment's garage building is of special interest with the diaper pattern in the brick adding a Deco touch to an otherwise utilitarian structure. The Bellevue Staten is important as an early work because Baumann adapted many of the cornice elements for use on his smaller-scale buildings in San

54. 1950 Clay Street, apartment building, designed by Herman C. Baumann, built in 1930; entry lobby. Photograph by Douglas Keister, Oakland, California.

56. *1700 Bay Street, apartment building, designed by Herman C. Baumann, built in 1936; entry lobby.*

55. *1950 Clay Street, apartment building, designed by Herman C. Baumann, built in 1930; mirror in entry lobby.*

Francisco, most notably on the apartment building at 1950 Clay Street built in 1930 (fig. 59).

Large apartment buildings were constructed throughout the thirties, with a brief hiatus during the early years of the Great Depression. Smaller residential flats buildings continued to show the influence of the style until the early fifties. These flats, residences, and smaller apartment buildings tended to be clustered at the corners of the major east-west streets, such as Judah, Taraval, and Fulton in the western reaches of the city (figs. 60, 61). The residences in the mid-sections of these blocks are generally earlier in construction date, because the lots would have been cheaper to build on. These corner buildings date from the mid-thirties, but elements of the style can still be found on buildings constructed as late as 1955.

San Francisco also has a rich variety of other kinds of Deco buildings including schools, theaters, neighborhood commercial buildings, and industrial buildings. James Lick Middle School, designed by William H. Crim in 1929 in Noe Valley, occupies an entire city block. The exterior has bas-reliefs and a perimeter fence with stepped concrete posts that reflect the building profile. The Vogue Theater at

57. *845 California Street, apartment building, designed by Herman C. Baumann, built in 1930; entry door and lantern.*

58. *492 Staten Street, Oakland, Bellevue Staten Apartments, designed by Herman C. Baumann, built in 1928-1929.*

Sacramento Street and Presidio, despite an altered lobby entrance, has a well-designed neon marquee and vertical sign integrated into the façade. Although Chestnut Street in the Marina contains the most concentrated collection of small commercial buildings, individual neighborhoods can usually boast of at least one polychrome terra-cotta storefront similar to these buildings. Most of the industrial buildings are located south of Market Street but others such as the Royal Baking Company building at 4769 Mission Street can be found elsewhere in the city (see fig. 4).

The city also has its monuments, such as Coit Tower atop Telegraph Hill. Constructed as a memorial to the firemen who were so important to the early history of the city, it is decorated with WPA murals that depict the city during this heady period. But towering literally and figuratively above all of the city is the largest Deco construction, the Golden Gate Bridge, completed in 1937. Joseph Strauss was the engineer, and the architect was Irving Morrow. In contrast to

59. 1950 Clay Street, apartment building, designed by Herman C. Baumann, built in 1930.

60. 1638-44 Judah Street, flats buildings, built in 1938; typical of the flats buildings found in many of the city's neighborhoods.

61. 4930 Fulton Street, apartment building, built in 1939; a typical apartment building found in many of the city's neighborhoods.

other monumental bridges constructed in other parts of the country during the period, the Golden Gate Bridge has architectural elements not found on the others. The concrete piers at the approach to the bridge appear to be mini-stepped skyscrapers taken from a Hugh Ferris drawing. The monumental bridge piers are stepped, and the arched openings in the piers have ornament inspired by Mayan architecture. The pier spandrels are enhanced with prism-like ornament taken directly from the Polish pavilion at the 1925 Exposition. Its size alone makes the Golden Gate Bridge one of the largest Art Deco structures anywhere in California.

San Francisco and the Bay Area possess a rich heritage of Deco buildings that make it a visually exciting place to live in, walk around, and above all, enjoy!

ART DECO PLASTER

There was a great deal of construction at the outset of the Art Deco period in San Francisco slowed by the Great Depression but continuing as early as 1931. Surprisingly, many of these building interiors still retain their original finishes and colors. For this reason they provide an invaluable source for understanding how these interiors are similar to or different from previous styles and periods.

The plaster finishes exhibit not only the characteristics of the Art Deco style but also show a high degree of importance in the overall decorative program used on the buildings. These finishes include molded colored-plaster ornament, pigment-infused plaster walls, raked and combed plaster work, and stenciling. In many instances all of these finishes were combined for stunning results (fig. 62).

62. 1750 Vallejo Street, apartment building; detail of the lobby ceiling showing molded, painted, and stenciled ornament.

Plaster, a highly plastic material, can take on many finishes, limited only by the architect's imagination, the skill of the artisan, and the client's needs and desires. The basic tools of the plasterer provided the ability to create these finishes. A raked or combed finish has a surface produced by the alteration of the smooth surface plaster coat by the action of dragging a rake or comb over it. This can produce a regularized surface or it can sometimes imitate a tooled ashlar finish, brick, or even textiles. Brooms were used to produce a faux-travertine finish. Brushes, rags, including burlap bags, and crumpled newspapers were also used to achieve a different look. Regular repeat patterns resulted from raking or pressing a hand-held form or stamp mold into the wet plaster. Sand was sometimes added to the base plaster or wash coat for additional texture; this is especially true when a stone finish was desired (figs. 63, 64).

Pigment was added by washes to the plaster in layers or directly to the ornament. In most instances it was mixed with the plaster to provide color integral to the plaster. In other instances a slightly different or contrasting color or colors were mixed in a plaster wash or applied in dabs to the wet plaster, then wiped off or otherwise distressed to reveal both color and pattern through the layers. The twenty-five or thirty different colors used were water-base colors. The surface could have a matte finish or

65. *1580 Beach Street, apartment building, built in 1931; detail of molded ornament on lobby walls with original rubbed colors.*

66. *1580 Beach Street, apartment building, built in 1931; detail of molded ornament on lobby walls with original rubbed colors.*

be glazed. A glazed finish was often used on molded ornament. Colors would be specified on the architectural drawings.

The molded ornament shown on architectural drawings was made by specially trained craftsmen, who also mounted the ornament (figs. 65, 66). They often retained the molds and as a result the same ornament can be found on buildings designed by different architects (figs. 67, 68, 69). Molded ornament was obtained through catalogs from manufacturers in San Francisco or Oakland and from as far away as New York and Philadelphia. These molded pieces were available in square-foot or yard-foot pieces as required.

Finishes were determined usually by the architect from samples furnished by the plasterer or sometimes left to the discretion of the plaster artisan. Some architects, notably Martin Rist, were known for standing next to the plasterer to approve the color and finish and requiring repeated applications before giving final approval for the job. The goal was to achieve an unusual and antique look. Although Art Deco was a "modern movement," in this instance the desire for richness and originality

67. 1695 Beach Street, apartment building, built in 1931; detail of lobby ceiling with molded-plaster ornament taken from German Expressionist graphics.

68. 1695 Beach Street, apartment building, built in 1931; detail of lobby ceiling with a molded-plaster ornament taken from German Expressionist sources, showing a crystal or prism that was emblematic of the movement.

69. 2090 Broadway, apartment building, designed by Herman C. Baumann, built in 1935; detail of molded-plaster ceiling ornament.

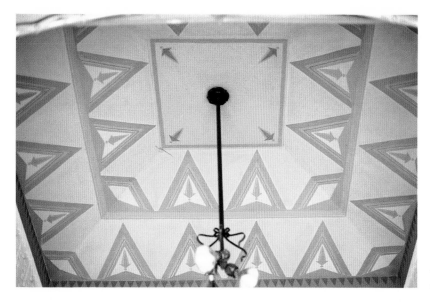

70. *1080 Eddy Street, apartment building, designed by Albert Larsen, built in 1929-1930; detail of stenciled ceiling in entry.*

71. *4930 Fulton Street, apartment building, built in 1939; detail of lobby ceiling showing molded and stenciled ceiling decoration with metallic paint.*

overrode the appearance of newness. The finishes and their variety are virtually limitless. This also testifies to their uniqueness. For the most part, only one or two plasterers would work on a specific interior because each had an individual style that would need to be consistent in one space.

Stenciling, an old decorative form, was used on flat surfaces both alone and with molded ornament to create a rich effect (figs. 70, 71, 72). The stencil forms are composed of relatively simple repeat patterns cut into templates used to draw the design on the flat plaster and then infilled with paint. The paint could be applied by hand or with an air brush for a different effect. Several colors could be used, each requiring a separate template keyed to the desired design. This paint was usually oil-base. It should be noted that these stenciled designs were far simpler than the more elaborate designs and complex color relationships of earlier Victorian stencils.

Stencils can be found in both the entry and the interior lobby on both the ceiling and the walls, augmenting and enhancing the molded plaster ornament. The stencil colors were the same as those used for the molded ornament. By the mid-

72. 1870 Pacific, apartment building, designed by Herman C. Baumann, built in 1937; detail of lobby ceiling showing molded and stenciled ceiling decoration with metallic paint.

thirties metallic paints such as gold and silver were popular, as were gold leaf, silver leaf, and copper leaf. Sometimes several of these colors were combined in one space.

The high-style buildings of Pflueger and Kelham provided the inspiration for and influence on what occurred in the interiors of the fashionable apartments constructed in Pacific Heights, the Marina, and Nob Hill. Variations of the lobby-ceiling design of the Stock Exchange Building (see figs. 36, 37) can be found on numerous buildings, including those at 640 Mason Street and 1790 Jackson Street (figs. 73, 74). The foundation for these techniques had been laid in the rich Victorian interiors of the preceding decades and also in the Spanish Colonial Revival-style buildings

73. *640 Mason Street, apartment building, designed by Herman C. Baumann, built in 1932; detail of molded-plaster ceiling ornament with metallic paint.*

that had begun to replace the relatively austere Classic Revival interiors by the early twenties.

By the late twenties the format of recessed entry with marble or bright tile work, entry door, tympanum, and sidelights with decorative grillwork; or an elaborate lobby, often two stories in height, featuring facing plate-glass mirrors with plaster surrounds, a decorative ceiling, and elaborate light fixtures was a part of the apartment-entry architectural vocabulary. Art Deco buildings elaborated on this format by introducing new forms, colors, and finishes for the plaster.

These Deco finishes, however, have not always received the respect accorded to their Victorian antecedents. The finishes have been subjected to all manner of abuse. Most common is repainting. The flat plaster is often painted a stark matte-white, thus radically changing the finish on the plaster, obscuring the decorative surface, and altering the quality of the space due to the color isolation of the glazed plaster ornament from the other wall surfaces. In other instances, the ornament is overpainted in the popular "Post Modern" pastels, changing the impact of the rich Deco colors.

74. 1790 Jackson Street, apartment building, designed by Herman C. Baumann, built in 1940; detail of molded-plaster ceiling ornament with metallic paint.

Restoration or rehabilitation techniques should follow sound methods for dealing with fragile materials. Harsh cleaning can cause loss of detailing; insensitive overpainting can change the appearance. Paint removal should be accomplished carefully and test patches should be used to evaluate the effect of paint strippers. Where only dirt removal is required it is important to evaluate the finish and determine if the finish is matte, glazed, or has some other special quality that would influence the method to be used in cleaning the surface. The exact nature of the paint may need to be analyzed to receive proper care and cleaning. This is true especially for stenciled work and metallic paints. Surfaces that are decorated with water-base paints or pigments could be altered by moisture penetration from liquid cleaners. Commercial products used for cleaning wallpaper may not be suitable for decorative plaster. Caution should be the watchword in trying to restore the historic finish.

IV ART DECO TERRA COTTA

Terra cotta was a popular building material during the Art Deco period for several reasons. The architects were familiar with the material and its use, which had been reintroduced in America in the later nineteenth century. It was especially popular at the turn of the century for use on Classic Revival-style buildings, favored during the City Beautiful movement. In San Francisco it was popular particularly after the 1906 disaster because terra cotta-clad buildings often came through the fire relatively unscathed. The best-known example is the Fairmont Hotel on Nob Hill, whose presence can be readily seen in many of the post-fire photographs from the period. Further, terra cotta could take on different kinds of finishes in imitation of other materials, and most important, color could be fused to it.

Terra cotta, which literally means baked earth and is reddish-brown in color, is made from clay and ground terra cotta. In a very labor-intensive manufacturing process, the mixture is forced into a plaster mold, is allowed to cure, and then fired in a kiln. Because it is lighter than stone, terra cotta requires a lighter structural system, so it was prized for highrise construction because of the lower costs involved. Terra cotta was available in California through several California manufacturers including Gladding McBean and N. Clark and Son.

Terra cotta also gained in popularity because the finish could imitate marble or granite. The best example is the War Memorial Opera House, which is terra cotta with a granite finish. But it was during the Art Deco period that architects began to expand its use because of the color capabilities. Pflueger's Telephone Company Building is typical of the early use where the color imitates a granite finish. His 450 Sutter Building and Kelham's Shell Building mark a move away from this tradition of imitating granite or marble. It should be noted that the use of color on buildings had been discussed a decade earlier in the writings of the German Expressionist architects. By the twenties and thirties American architects were taking this to heart.

In the I. Magnin Building by Weeks and Day at the corner of 20th and Broadway in Oakland we see the full expression of the effect colored terra cotta can have. This building, in a rich medium blue-green, has a highly molded surface with ornamentation in the shape of zigzags and stylized fountains in the window spandrels (fig. 75). But it is the color of the building that has the greatest impact. Variations of green can be found on other buildings such as the former John Bruener Co. Building (fig. 76) at 2201 Broadway, and the Anna Merriam Building, also in Oakland, at 347 14th Street. The other spectacular example in Oakland is the commercial building at the corner of 19th and Telegraph that has an unusual navy-blue and silver color scheme, which required a special two-fire process in the manufacturing (fig. 77).

75. *2001-2011 Broadway, Oakland, I. Magnin & Co. Building, designed by Weeks and Day, built in 1931; detail of façade showing decorative terra-cotta in the window spandrels. Photograph by Douglas Keister, Oakland, California.*

76. *2201 Broadway, Oakland, former John Bruener Co. Building, designed by Albert F. Roller, built in 1931; detail showing the decorative terra cotta on the façade. Photograph by Douglas Keister, Oakland, California.*

In San Francisco, the popularity of color, especially all shades of green, can be found on the buildings at 200 Powell Street, the medical building at 5001 Geary Boulevard, and the storefront at 200–216 Powell (fig. 78).

Terra-cotta veneers were also used. This form of cladding differs from architectural terra cotta in that it is thinner, lighter in weight, and can be applied directly to surfaces such as concrete or plaster on wood lath. These tiles could be used on both exteriors such as storefronts and on interiors, usually in bathrooms or kitchens. The colors ran the full range of the rainbow. One of the best examples is a

small market at 820 Bush Street on Nob Hill (figs. 79, 80). This little building manages to combine red, green, and yellow-gold tiles in forms that create visual excitement. The brace-shaped profile of the dark green tile is a standard shape that also came in a range of colors, including dark red, pale jade green, navy blue, yellow, peach, orange, and black (fig. 81). Most often the tile can be found on small commercial buildings, but one of the most unusual examples was the Whitehurst-Shannon Funeral Home in Modesto, California, which unfortunately has been demolished. There peach and maroon tiles were highlighted with jade-green tiles.

Usually, the color on buildings during this period was reserved for the areas of terra-cotta cladding such as decorative panels around the doorway and entrance (figs. 82, 83, 84). Of course, the material could be used for remodeling, which became popular for older buildings. Examples of this use can be found at 2000 Chestnut Street, which unfortunately has been painted, and 2231 Chestnut. Unless there was polychrome terra cotta or black-glass trim, most buildings were monochromatic in color, with white, off-white, cream, or gray being the most popular colors (figs. 85, 86, 87).

77. 1900-32 Telegraph Avenue, Oakland, commercial building, designed by Albert J. Evers, built in 1931; detail showing tower in navy-blue and silver terra cotta. Photograph by Douglas Keister, Oakland, California.

78. 200-216 Powell Street, commercial building, built in 1933; showing the green terra-cotta cladding favored during the period.

79. *826 Bush Street, commercial building; an example of polychrome terra-cotta veneer.*

80. *826 Bush Street, commercial building; detail of polychrome terra-cotta veneer.*

81. 1943-55 Lawton Street, commercial building; detail of terra-cotta veneer showing brace-shaped tile.

82. 1935-39 Lawton Street, commercial building; detail of polychrome terra-cotta veneer.

83. 1733 Polk Street, commercial/residential building, built in 1907, Art Deco-ized about 1930; detail of polychrome tile in entry.

84. 425 Grant Avenue, commercial building; façade.

85. 1850 Gough Street, apartment building, designed by L. O. Ebbetts, built in 1930; detail of polychrome tile in entry.

86. 3030 Cabrillo Street, apartment building, built in 1930; detail of polychrome tile in entry.

87. 3740-50 24th Street, apartment building, built in 1904, Art Deco-ized about 1930–1935; detail of polychrome tile in entry.

▼ NEON

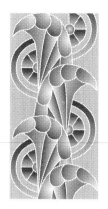

Both a Frenchman and a German are credited with independently discovering the process for making pure oxygen. As a result of this process, rare gases, one of which is neon, were produced. However, it was Georges Claude, the Frenchman, who developed a cheap extraction process for oxygen. But he had no use for the leftover rare gases until he came across a Moore tube, an early type of luminous-tube light. Claude found that by filling a glass tube with neon and bombarding it with electricity he was able to produce a clear intense red; with argon he produced a grayish blue.

With this process Claude took the first steps in the formation of the luminous-tube industry. In 1919, the main entrance of the Paris Opera was lit with Claude neon in orange and blue to create an effect that came to be known as "les couleurs Opéra," thus establishing the popularity of this color scheme for the next two decades.

The first neon sign in the United States was erected in Los Angeles. In 1923, Earle C. Anthony imported two signs from Paris made of Claude Neon. At a cost of $1,250, they were simple signs of orange letters spelling "Packard" and surrounded by a blue border. So the popularity of the "Couleurs Opéra" were established with the first sign in the United States.

Claude began franchising the method for making his long-life electrode in 1924. Franchises were sold in San Francisco and other major cities in the country. However, the method of making signs, called bending, was quickly learned, and manufacturers began producing signs without benefit of Claude's franchise.

Initially, signs were additive to buildings—that is, the sign was added to the exterior of an already existing building. This was intended to give the building a new modern look, which became especially important with the onset of the Great Depression. A good example of this type of sign is the Senator Hotel sign at 519 Ellis Street (fig. 88).

Signs were located on different parts of a building: a fascia sign lies flat against the building, a vertical sign can be attached at the corners or along the façade. Rooftop signs could be either billboard types or individual letters such as the sign for the Huntington Hotel on Nob Hill. Sometimes pole signs were added to the roof. The best example of this type is located next to 2200 Mission Street, but unfortunately, it is no longer working.

Examples of additive signs abound in the Tenderloin. Many of the residential hotels of the Tenderloin had been built for the 1915 Panama-Pacific International Exposition held on reclaimed land in the Marina. By the time neon signs were introduced in San Francisco, it was time for these hotels to need a spruce up, and what better way to add a truly modern touch than with a neon sign? In addition to the Senator Hotel, the Essex Hotel at 684 Ellis is another example.

88. 519 Ellis Street, Senator Hotel; neon sign added about 1928.

Neon tubing was added or signs were attached to an existing marquee or an entirely new neon marquee would be installed on a building. This is particularly true in the case of theaters. The Castro, Royal, and Alhambra theaters were designed by Timothy Pflueger in 1922, 1928, and 1929 respectively. The present signs and marquees, designed by Alexander Aimwell Cantin, were added in 1935 (see figs. 41, 45, 46).

By the early thirties the use of neon was beginning to be integrated into the overall building design. Cantin went on to design the Orinda Theater in Orinda, California, which is one of the best examples of the integration of a sign with the façade of a building (fig. 89). Built in 1940–1941, the façade shows the influence of Pflueger's Royal Theater of 1928 and the buildings of the 1939 Golden Gate

89. Moraga Way, Orinda; Orinda Theater, designed by Alexander Aimwell Cantin, built in 1941; example of integration of vertical sign into façade design.

International Exposition, especially the towers flanking the Court of the Moon. There are other examples on a lesser scale, notably Victor's Market at 2324 Chestnut Street, designed by Herman C. Baumann and built in 1937 with an inventive use of recessed neon tubing so that the name is the sole design element on the façade (see fig. 114). Other good theater examples are the Vogue Theater at Sacramento and Presidio (fig. 90), the Grand Theater at 2665 Mission Street, the New Mission Theater at 2550 Mission Street by Timothy Pflueger, and the Bridge Theater at 3008 Geary Boulevard. The last has one of the few remaining sequentially lighting signs.

The box of the sign holds the transformer and its surface often carries out the color scheme established in the colors used in the neon letters. The Curran Theater sign at 445 Geary is an example of this type of sign (fig. 91). In an unusual touch it has a wreath of recessed neon tubing to give a soft green edge surrounding the letters. The box also has very fine painted details in Streamline style. Another example of recessed lighting is the sign on the Bi Rite Liquor store on 18th Street, where the back-lit letters cast an alluring glow over the terra-cotta facing (fig. 92).

There are many notable examples of signs through the city with some of the more elaborate uses of building outlining in Chinatown. The sign on the Great Star Theater at 630 Jackson Street is a very early sign from about 1930 (fig. 93). The stepped shape made by the green neon border at the top and bottom is an indication of its early date. Often the shaped ends were complemented with additional neon ornament above or below the letters. By the mid-thirties the shape of the box had changed when rounded and more streamlined forms became the norm.

90. *Sacramento Street at Presidio, Vogue Theater; example of integration of vertical sign into façade design.*

91. *445 Geary Street, Curran Theater, neon sign added about 1935; good example of design elements on the box and creative use of recessed tubing.*

92. *18th Street, Bi Rite Liquors; neon sign with backlit letters.*

93. *630 Jackson, Great Star Theater, neon sign added about 1928; one of numerous signs and tubing added to buildings in Chinatown throughout the twenties and thirties.*

VI ART DECO·IZED BUILDINGS

It's not surprising that many buildings were "updated" and given a veneer of Art Deco ornament. This occurred on all types of buildings from simple stores to highrises and private homes. Especially after the Great Depression set in, it was one way to give a building a new look and therefore make it more desirable to work in, live in, or shop in. In addition, with the curtailing of new construction work because of the economy this was often the only work available for architects.

Highrise structures had ornament stripped off and smooth stucco replaced once highly articulated elevations as with the Central Tower at 703 Market Street, which was remodeled by Albert Roller in 1938 (fig. 94). The firm of Hyman and Appleton gave a more traditional look to the building at 343 Sansome, where the stepped upper floors and the splayed entry were finished in subtly colored terra cotta (fig. 95).

These kinds of changes worked very well and point up the skill that many architects used in making the changes. However, not all changes were so well designed. The nineteenth-century house at 389 Oak Street received an improbable Deco veneer when the Victorian-style ornament was stripped and replaced with stucco (fig. 96). But this treatment does point out the essential elements that someone considered sufficient to convey the style. The stepped piers flanking the entry and diamonds at the cornice are now picked out in color to add to the look.

The molded-plaster ornament created by architects for high-style apartment buildings could often find its way to a residential building because of the plaster artisan. This is probably the case in the building at 1836-38 Greenwich. There are several other buildings, located at 3119 Jackson, 2122 Lake (fig. 97), 678 Haight, and 2170 Vallejo (fig. 98), which received virtually identical ornament. The treatments are successful despite the differences in the individual buildings.

Storefronts often were altered with a polychrome terrazzo entry, pigmented glass bulkhead, often splayed or faceted, with stepped lights in the entry door, and sometimes a complementary neon sign. Terra cotta also provided the means to add color and ornament to a façade, which is the case at 742-48 Grant Avenue. The Chestnut Street Bar and Grille at 2231 Chestnut Street and Drewes Meat Market at 1704 Church Street are other good examples of these attempts at modernization. As shown in these illustrations, the variations on updating a building could take many interesting forms (figs. 99, 100).

94. 703 Market Street, Central Tower Building, built in 1898; remodeled by Albert Roller in 1938.

95. 343 Sansome Street, former Crown-Zellerbach Building, remodeled by Hyman and Appleton in 1930.

96. 389 Oak Street, house, built about 1885, remodeled about 1935.

97. 2122 Lake Street, house, remodeled about 1935.

98. 2170 Vallejo Street, house, remodeled about 1935.

99. *1770 Pacific Street, apartment building, built 1902, remodeled about 1930.*

100. *50 Frederick Street, apartment building, remodeled about 1935–1940.*

VII PRESERVATION IN SAN FRANCISCO

Preservation is an important issue in San Francisco. Unfortunately, this concern has not always protected Art Deco buildings. In recent years, large buildings, such as the former Falstaff Brewery at 10th and Folsom (fig. 101), and small ones, such as the gas station at Jackson and Montgomery Street (fig. 102), have been demolished. Neither of the buildings was a landmark, so protection and concern were limited. However, the gas station originally located at Pacific and Larkin (fig. 103) was denied a demolition request by the Landmarks Board. The Foundation for San Francisco's Architectural Heritage has since made arrangements for the structure to be moved to a new site.

There have been successes, however. The Orinda Theater was saved from demolition and has been restored, including the murals in the lobby and on the auditorium walls (fig. 104). The Alameda Theater still faces an uncertain future. Inappropriately used as a gymnastics studio, all of the seats and some of the light fixtures have been removed. It had been selected as the site for a new library. However, there is strong community sentiment, with the support of the Art Deco Society of California, to retain the building so that a more appropriate alternative use or a return to its original use can be developed.

The San Francisco Landmarks Preservation Advisory Board has taken steps in its designation guidance for Chinatown to protect the neon signs and Art Deco storefronts found on many of the buildings in the proposed historic district. But the designation has not been enacted. It can't come too soon, for the finely detailed Deco storefront at 425 Grant Avenue was completely removed just a few years ago. In late 1989, an original storefront at 943 Market Street that dated from 1930 was demolished, including the original polychrome terrazzo entry floor, tile bulkheads, doors, and light fixtures. The new business remained in operation for only a year.

Recently, the Treasure Island Museum Society has begun a fund-raising effort to restore the sculptures (figs. 105, 106) installed on the Island as part of the 1939–1940 World's Fair. In addition, a terra-cotta fountain that depicts the Pacific basin in bas-relief will be moved to a new location in front of the Museum building.

All of this speaks of a lack of appreciation or understanding of the importance of the architecture from the period. The Art Deco Society of California (100 Bush Street, Suite 511, San Francisco, California 94104, phone (415) 982-DECO) has encouraged and participated in many of the preservation efforts. It carries out a program of public education through lectures and walking tours for the general public to help spread the appreciation of and interest in the Art Deco architecture of the San Francisco Bay Area.

101. 10th Street and Folsom, former Falstaff Brewery Building, reinforced concrete, demolished.

102. Montgomery Street, gas station, demolished.

103. 1501 Pacific, gas station, moved.

104. Moraga Way, Orinda;
Orinda Theater, designed by
Alexander Aimwell Cantin, built
in 1941; detail showing paint-
ings on lobby ceiling.

105, 106. Treasure Island; concrete sculptures awaiting
restoration and relocation.

VIII WALKING TOURS

The walking tours are arranged so that the number on the map refers to the written entry. By following the numbers on the map you can determine the actual walking route. There are general comments about the building noting the prominent features. But as with any walking tour it's not just the building itself that you should be looking at but also the details such as house numbers, mailboxes, fire escapes, and light fixtures that often provide surprises because of their originality (fig. 107).

107. 1900 Beach Street, apartment building, designed by Herman C. Baumann, built in 1936; detail of entrance.

Marina Walking Tour

The Marina is built on fill that was first dumped in the area after the earthquake and fire of 1906. In 1915, this area, known as Harbor View, was selected as the site of the Panama-Pacific International Exposition (PPIE), and the filling of the marshes and salt flats was accelerated. After the PPIE the land was developed as one of the newest residential areas of the city. The buildings cited on the tour are not the only Art Deco buildings in the Marina. You are encouraged to explore the area on your own and discover the delightful residences and apartment buildings. Many of the entries and lobbies still retain their original tile, stenciling, light fixtures, and carpets. Enjoy!

1. 2000 Chestnut.
Formerly the Anglo-American Bank, built in 1927, remodeled in 1934 by S. Heiman; had green, black, and silver terra cotta on the first floor. After the 1989 earthquake the terra cotta was painted black.

2. 2026 Chestnut.
Commercial building, built in 1934; has terra-cotta tile near the cornice and incised-plaster floral motifs that are vaguely Egyptian in style.

3. 2030-34 Chestnut.
Commercial building, built in 1934; has original shopfronts, doors, light fixtures, and decorative tile bulkhead with zigzag motif.

4. 2040 Chestnut.
Commercial building, former Safeway, designed by Ellison and Russell, and built in 1933; design based on the Galeries Lafayette Pavilion at the 1925 Paris Exposition (fig. 108).

5. 2066-68 Chestnut.
Commercial building, built in 1933; has decorative cornice line with Mayan-style slant-arch windows.

6. 2080 Chestnut.
Commercial building, built in 1933; the pale green and silver terra-cotta tile and neon sign are original (fig. 109).

108. 2040 Chestnut Street, commercial building.

109. 2086-90 Chestnut Street, commercial building.

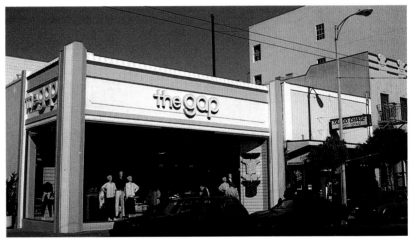

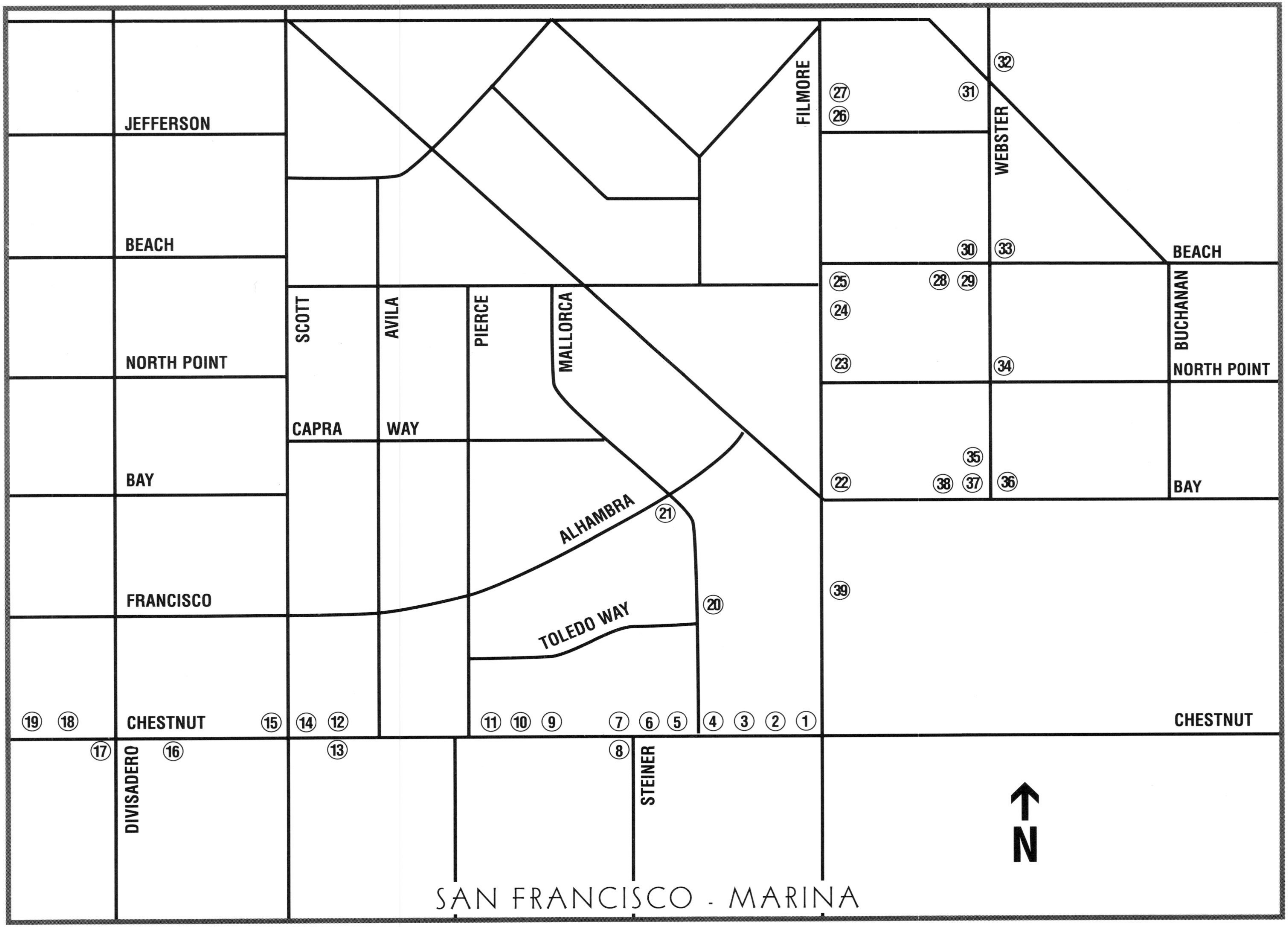

SAN FRANCISCO · MARINA

N→

DIVISADERO

CHESTNUT

FRANCISCO

BAY

NORTH POINT

BEACH

JEFFERSON

CAPRA

SCOTT

WAY

AVILA

PIERCE

TOLEDO WAY

ALHAMBRA

MALLORCA

STEINER

FILMORE

WEBSTER

CHESTNUT

BAY

NORTH POINT

BUCHANAN

BEACH

110. 2124-30 Chestnut Street, commercial building.

111. 2124-30 Chestnut Street, commercial build-ing.

7. 2088 Chestnut.

Commercial building, built in 1931; the stained-glass sunburst tran-soms are original, although the matching transom to the right is blocked, alas.

8. 3345 Steiner.

Restaurant, a former U.S. Post Office, built in 1936; the decorative stylized eagles at the cornice and curved window reveals show the influence of Cubism and streamlining.

9. 2124-30 Chestnut.

Commercial building, built in 1932; note the sunray design on the façade. Sees Candies shop is in near-original condition with light fix-tures, counters, clock, etc., still intact—amazing (figs. 110, 111).

10. 2150 Chestnut.

Commercial building, built in 1932; has decorative marquee and Mayan-style transom windows.

11. 2174-76 Chestnut.

Commercial building, built in 1931; has molded plaster decoration and floral grilles. Unfortunately, the green and silver terra-cotta trim has been painted white (fig. 112).

112. 2176 Chestnut Street, commercial building.

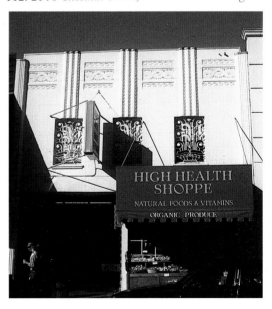

113. 2250 Chestnut Street, commercial building.

114. 2324 Chestnut Street, Victor's Market.

115. 50 Mallorca Street, flats building.

12. 2220-30 Chestnut.

Commercial building, built in 1933; has molded-plaster ornament at cornice level and polychrome terrazzo at the shop entries.

13. 2231 Chestnut.

Chestnut Street Grille, built in 1914 and remodeled about 1934; has green stenciled terra-cotta tiles that match the incised tiles at 2000 Chestnut. The back bar on the interior still remains.

14. 2240-48 Chestnut.

Commercial building, built in 1931; has terra-cotta tiles, some of which are painted, and polychrome terrazzo at each shop entry.

15. 2250 Chestnut.

Commercial building, designed by Francis E. Floyd, and built in 1933; has unusual cornice decoration, green terra-cotta trim, and curved storefront windows (fig. 113).

16. 2255 Chestnut.

Commercial building, built about 1935; has original stepped cornice and splayed neon sign.

17. 2301-23 Chestnut.

Commercial building, designed by Alex Stern, and built in 1931; has cast-plaster floral decoration recently restored to the original color scheme.

18. 2324 Chestnut.

Victor's Market, designed by Herman C. Baumann, and built in 1937; displays an inventive use of neon that makes the shop name the primary design element on the façade (fig. 114).

19. 2340 Chestnut.

Presidio Theater, designed by John H. Ahnden, and built in 1937; has pulvinated speed lines and original neon-lit marquee and shopfronts.

20. 50 Mallorca.

Flats building, built in 1941; has incised stepped lines at the cornice, curved façade bays, and vertical prism details (fig. 115).

21. 165 Mallorca.

Apartment building, built in 1938; has curved façade, marble entry floor with rays, and original blue mirrors and light fixtures in the lobby.

22. 3632 Fillmore.

Residence, built in 1936; has Expressionist-style ornament under the bay window, splayed window reveals, and a stylized floral panel on the façade.

23. 3650 Fillmore.
Apartment building, designed by R.R. Irvine, and built in 1933; a "proto-Deco" building with incised stepped lines in the window spandrels.

24. 3720 Fillmore.
Apartment building, built in 1931; has molded-plaster ornament at the cornice and decorative fire escapes. A remodeling of the lobby has removed all the Art Deco detailing.

25. 3740 Fillmore.
Apartment building, built in 1933; has decorative grilles at entry door and sidelights.

26. 1490 Jefferson.
Apartment building, designed by R.R. Irvine, and built in 1931; has notable polychrome entry tiles and molded-plaster ornament in the lobby.

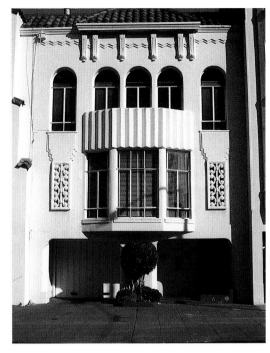

116. 3760 Fillmore Street, flats building.

27. 3760-62 Fillmore.
Flats building, built in 1932; has zigzag cornice detail, faceted bay-window spandrels, stepped plaster façade ornament, and Mayan-inspired grilles (fig. 116).

28. 1695 Beach.
Apartment building, built in 1931, and possibly designed by R.R. Irvine; has bright polychrome entry tiles, molded and stenciled plaster ornament on the lobby ceiling, and canted muntin bars in the windows.

29. 1601 Beach.
Apartment building, built in 1935; has a split personality. Although the exterior is Spanish Colonial Revival in style, the entry and lobby are splendid Art Deco.

30. 1600 Beach.
Apartment building, built in 1936; has Bakelite insets on the façade, zigzag plaster details over the entry, and the original carpet on the entry stairs.

31. 3757 Webster.
Apartment building, designed by R.R. Irvine, and built in 1934; has notable lobby and entry, unusual light fixtures built into the entry arch, similar to buildings at Divisadero and the 2400 block of Fulton Street. Note the Chinese Deco table in the lobby.

32. 3780 Webster.
Residence, built in 1937, and possibly designed by Herman C. Baumann; has zigzag detailing at the cornice, stepped Mayan-arch entry, and curved bays. The portion on the upper left of the second floor is a later addition of about 1985.

33. 1580 Beach.

Apartment building, built in 1931, and possibly designed by R.R. Irvine; has an outstanding combed-plaster lobby with the original color scheme intact—wow!

34. 1680 North Point.

Apartment building, designed by Herman C. Baumann and built in 1937; has molded plaster at the entry, a stepped entry arch, a pantile roof with molded-plaster plaques, and decorative fire escapes and window grilles.

35. 3639-41 Webster.

Flats, built in 1932; has decorative railings, stylized floral plaques, light fixtures, and doors.

36. 1690 Bay.

Apartment building, built in 1936; has a stenciled lobby ceiling, light fixtures still intact, and unusual color in the entry tiles.

37. 1700 Bay.

Apartment building, built in 1936; has glass-block insets, a stenciled lobby ceiling, and unusual plaster light sconces (fig. 117; see also fig. 56).

38. 1738-40-44-46 Bay.

Two very similar flats buildings, built in 1937; have decorative plaster plaques and stylized pilasters.

39. 3500 Fillmore.

Marina Middle School, designed by George Kelham and Will P. Day, and built in 1936; its style is "Greco Deco" with bronze transom grilles at the auditorium, "reverse" pilasters, and decorative roundels with lions, rams, bears, and maidens (see fig. 48).

117. 1700 Bay Street, apartment building.

Pacific Heights Walking Tour

Pacific Heights has undergone a great deal of change since the 1906 earthquake and fire. The area was spared fire damage but more recent changes in lifestyles and pressure for development has brought its own form of damage. This tour focuses on the apartment buildings built during the Art Deco period. Many of the buildings are architect-designed and show the "signature marks" of the architect. The buildings are notable for the inventive ornament, rich materials used in the lobbies, and the good state of preservation. There are many such apartment buildings in other areas of the city awaiting your discovery and enjoyment.

1. 1850 Gough.
Apartment building, designed by L.O. Ebbetts, and built in 1931; has a stylized daffodil and zigzag frieze (see also the commercial building at 19th and Mission), and decorative molded-plaster window spandrels. The polychrome entry has unusual silver, black, yellow, and orange tiles, a sunray transom grille, and an outstanding lobby with mirrors and a molded-plaster ceiling.

2. 1900 Gough.
Apartment building, built in 1937, and possibly designed by Irvine and Ebbetts; has molded-plaster floral window spandrels, a Mayan-style entry arch with marble wainscot, a decorative transom and sidelight grilles, and a lobby with mirrors, molded-plaster ornament, and Mayan-arched doorways (figs. 118, 119).

3. 1909 Sacramento.
Apartment building, designed by Herman C. Baumann, and built in 1930. Many of the original details remain, including the light fixtures at the entry, the "Stock Exchange Building" ceiling, and unusual scored-plaster lobby walls.

4. 1963-1981 Clay.
Three flats buildings, built in 1938; have streamline details such as glass-block insets, curved walls, corner windows, and porthole windows in the garage doors.

118. 1900 Gough Street, apartment building.

119. 1900 Gough Street, apartment building; detail showing entrance.

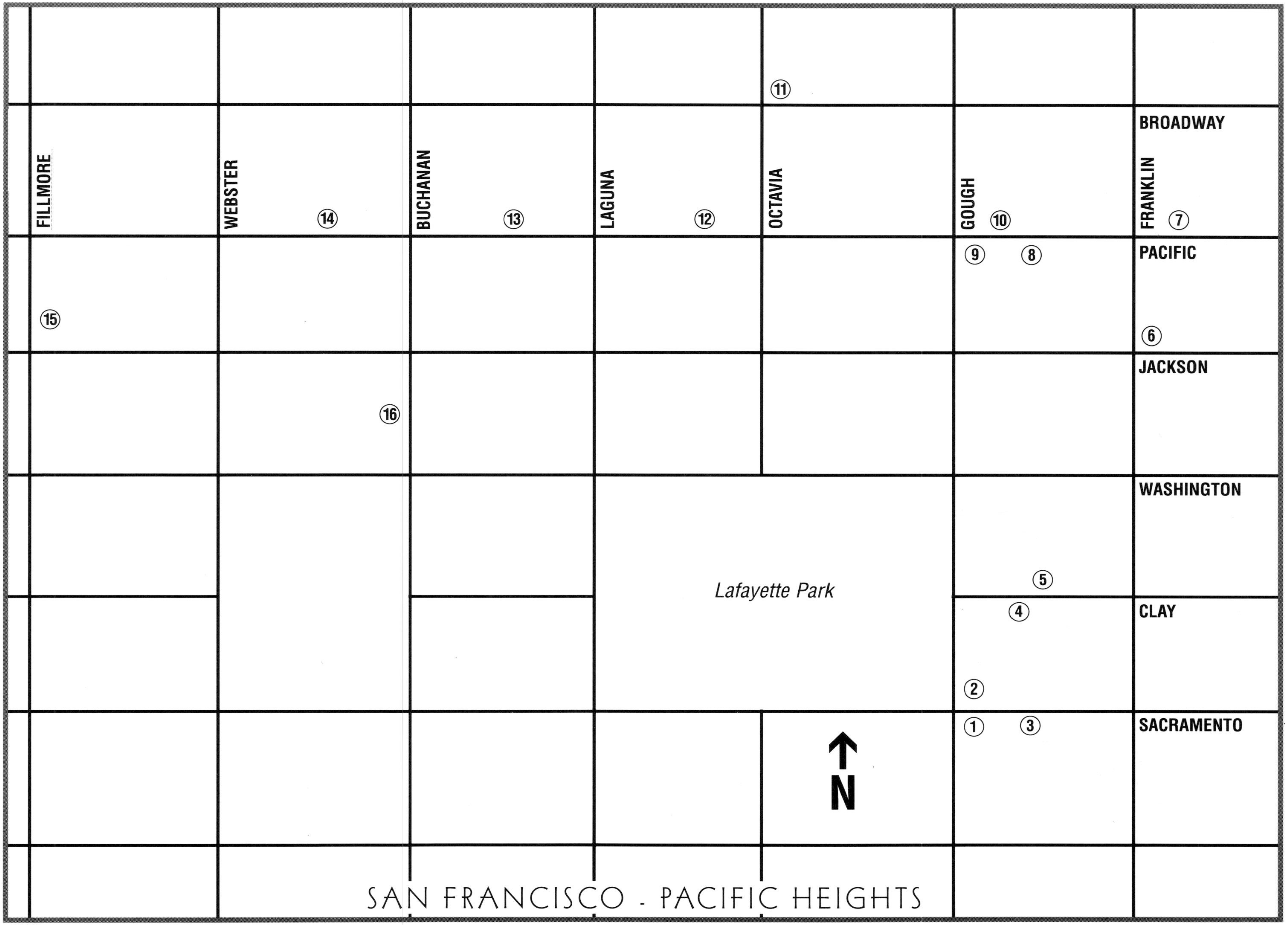

SAN FRANCISCO · PACIFIC HEIGHTS

N →

Lafayette Park

FILLMORE ⑮

WEBSTER ⑭

⑯

BUCHANAN ⑬

LAGUNA ⑫

OCTAVIA ⑪

GOUGH ⑨ ⑩ ⑧

① ②
④
③ ⑤

SACRAMENTO

CLAY

WASHINGTON

JACKSON ⑥

PACIFIC

FRANKLIN ⑦

BROADWAY

120. *1950 Clay Street, apartment building.*

5. 1950 Clay.
Apartment building, designed by Herman C. Baumann, and built in 1930. The exterior has molded-plaster window spandrels, Mayan-arched entry, and unique cornice ornament. The splendid lobby has a second-level opening, a Baumann trait, mirrors, and a stenciled ceiling with chevrons and zigzags in the original colors and plaster finish. The garage is flanked by shrubs clipped to complement the plaster ornament on the building (fig. 120).

6. 1790 Jackson.
Apartment building, designed by Herman C. Baumann, and built in 1940. The exterior is simply detailed with a vertical emphasis. The restrained lobby has marble ray motifs in the entry floor, a molded-plaster cornice, and "Stock Exchange Building" molded-plaster ceiling (see fig. 74).

7. 1770 Pacific.
Apartment building, built in 1902 and Art Deco-ized about 1930 with molded-plaster ornament in the window spandrels and restrained lobby decoration.

8. 1855 Pacific.
Apartment building, built in 1939, and possibly designed by L.O. Ebbetts. There are rays at the cornice and an outstanding entry and lobby. The entry has an orange-and-black marble wainscot. The lobby is divided into three areas—a square, an oval, and another square section—and it has a marvelous stenciled ceiling, original light fixtures, and an unusual porthole-shape mirror with pulvinated speed lines (fig. 121).

9. 1895 Pacific.
Apartment building, designed by Herman C. Baumann, and built in 1931; has Mayan-style arches at the entry and at the garages. The exterior has notable geometric-style molded ornament. The entry is distinguished by the sunray and floral grilles at the door, transom, and sidelights. The lobby has mirrors, a molded-plaster ceiling, recessed light niches, and original light fixtures. Unfortunately, the entry light fixtures have been replaced.

121. *1895 Pacific Street, apartment building; detail of lobby. Photograph by Douglas Keister, Oakland, California.*

10. 1870 Pacific.

Apartment building, designed by Herman C. Baumann, and built in 1937. The exterior is enlivened with plaster ornament culminating in flowerpot-like ornament possibly inspired by the ornament on the Pacific Telephone Company Building. The fire escape is integrated with the entrance canopy of the Mayan-style entry arch. The door and sidelights have decorative grilles. The interior lobby ceiling is stenciled and painted with metallic gold paint. The planter at the entrance may have been a fountain.

122. 2090 Broadway, apartment building.

11. 2090 Broadway.

Apartment building, designed by Herman C. Baumann, and built in 1935. It has a zigzag cornice, and the floral ornament on the balcony above the entry reflects the floral ornament used in the entry transom and sidelights. The lobby has an unusual circular plan with marble-clad walls and a molded-plaster ceiling. The light fixture was salvaged from the nineteenth-century house that was demolished when the new building was constructed on the site (figs. 122, 123).

123. 2090 Broadway, apartment
building; detail showing
entrance.

12. 2230-2250 Pacific.

Four two-flat buildings, built in 1949; have Mayan-inspired, stepped-cornice detailing and speed-line balcony railings at 2250.

13. 2340 Pacific.

Apartment building, built in 1932, and possibly designed by Herman C. Baumann. The exterior has "love bird" capitals on the entry pilasters, floral window spandrels, and a fire escape integrated with the entry canopy. Unfortunately, all of the lobby plaster ornament has been overpainted in a stark flat white.

14. 2360 Pacific.

Apartment building built in 1929 with a split personality, for there is a Spanish Colonial Revival entry, but the upper floors are trimmed in Art Deco terra cotta. The small-paned industrial sash is unusual on a domestic building.

15. 2500 Fillmore.

Commercial building, built in 1932, and is possibly a former Safeway. It is distinguished by molded-plaster ornament on the exterior and the interior, which is further enhanced with polychrome tilework on the walls behind the refrigerators.

16. 2425 Buchanan.

Apartment building, built in 1931, and possibly designed by Irvine and Ebbetts with rays, rays, and more rays on the entry grilles, garage doors, and fire escape. The entry has brilliant polychrome tiles. The lobby has a molded-plaster ceiling, zigzag detailing on the original light fixtures, and a niche with a light fixture (figs. 124, 125).

124. 2425 Buchanan Street, apartment building.

125. 2425 Buchanan Street, apartment building; detail of lobby.

Downtown San Francisco Walking Tour

San Francisco, like the phoenix on its city flag, rose triumphantly from the ashes of the 1906 earthquake and fire. The downtown retail and financial districts, although severely damaged by the fire, were virtually rebuilt by 1915. However, this did not prevent the later construction of significant Art Deco buildings, which are scattered over the entire downtown area.

1. 450 Sutter.

450 Sutter Building, designed by Timothy Pflueger, and built in 1928. This medical-arts building was the first to be built in the Mayan Revival style in San Francisco. The terracotta exterior has incised Mayan ornament and an unusual entry canopy. The lobby has dark marble walls and a stepped-plaster ceiling with incised ornament. The silver-color elevator doors also have incised Mayan decorative motifs. The light fixtures were added just a few years ago (see figs. 31–34).

2. 233 Geary Street.

I. Magnin Department Store, built in 1907, and redesigned by Timothy Pflueger and his brother Milton in 1946. The remodeling shows how the principles of the International Style, just emerging in this country, was beginning to replace Art Deco. However, the interior light fixtures show the continued use of Art Deco elements.

126. 491-499 Geary Street, Redwood Room at Clift Hotel. Photograph by Douglas Keister, Oakland, California.

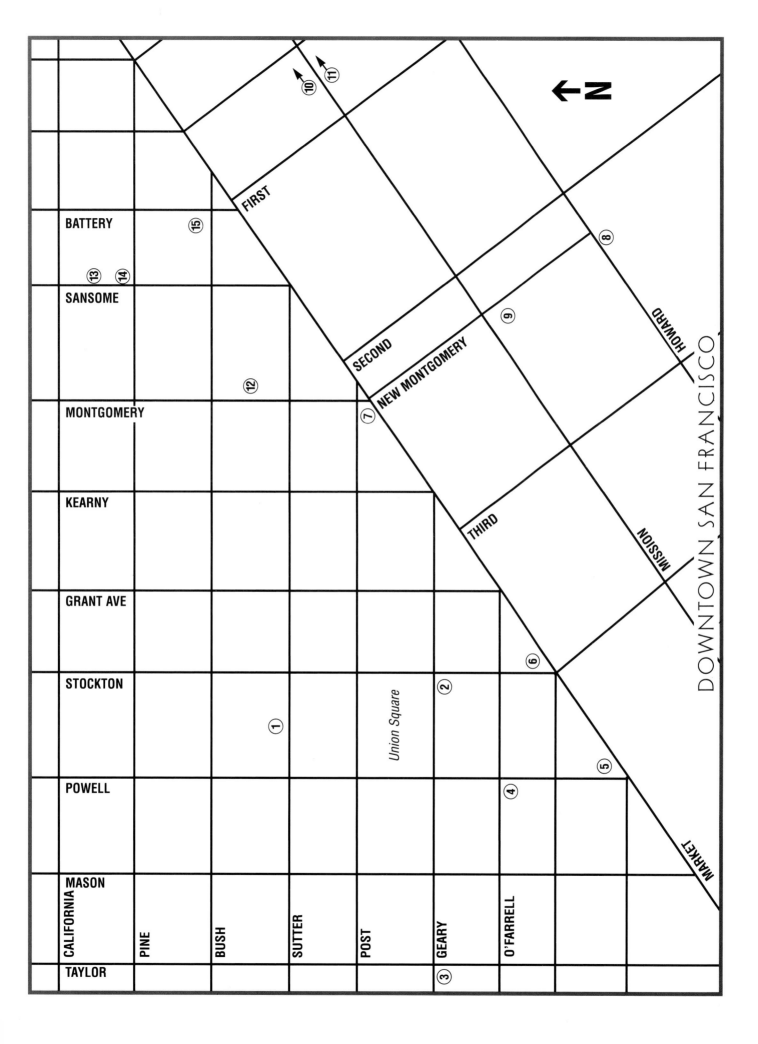

DOWNTOWN SAN FRANCISCO

3. 491-499 Geary Street.

Clift Hotel, built in 1913, and designed by MacDonald & Applegarth. An addition to the hotel, designed by Schultze & Weaver, was built in 1926. The Clift contains one of the great interior spaces in San Francisco—the Redwood Room (fig. 126), designed by G. A. Lansburgh and Anthony Heinsbergen, which is featured on the front of this book.

4. 200-216 Powell.

Commercial building, built in 1933. The jade-green terra-cotta exterior has been altered at the cornice, but many of the other details remain.

5. 790 Market Street.

Commercial building, built in 1907, and remodeled in 1937 by the firm of Bliss and Fairweather. The smooth terra-cotta exterior and very restrained ornament reflect the popularity of streamlining.

6. 703 Market Street.

Central Tower Building, built in 1898, and remodeled by Albert Roller in 1938. The original building was a Beaux Arts-style survivor of the 1906 fire with a very elaborate domed roof. The lobby contains remnants of the 1938 remodeling, such as marble walls, elevator interiors, and mailbox. The first-floor exterior was remodeled in 1988.

7. 140 New Montgomery Street.

Pacific Telephone Company Building, designed by Timothy Pflueger with Alexander Aimwell Cantin in 1926. It is the first building in the city to show the beginnings of the Art Deco style. The exterior terra-cotta cladding has been recently restored and replaced. Unusual exterior ornament abounds: eagles, bluebells, and "flying phone books." The interior lobby has marble walls and a spectacular plaster ceiling with Chinese motifs (see figs. 26–30).

8. 631 Howard Street.

William Volker Building, designed by George Kelham, and built in 1929. This low red-brick building with restrained cast-cement ornament provides a fitting terminus for the view down New Montgomery Street.

9. 425 Mission Street.

Transbay Terminal, designed by several architects, Timothy Pflueger, Arthur Brown, Jr., and John J. Donovan. It was built in 1939 to provide a terminus for the streetcars arriving via the newly completed Oakland–San Francisco Bay bridge. The windows hark back to another Pflueger design, the Stock Exchange Building at 155 Sansome Street.

10. 90 Mission Street.

Rincon Center, the former Rincon Annex Post Office, designed by Gilbert Stanley Underwood, and built in 1940. Although no longer functioning as a post office, the building has been incorporated into a new highrise development. Most of the exterior details remain, including diving dolphins, eagles, and the Deco-style lettering. The lobby interior features terra-cotta walls, light fixtures, and murals by Anton Refriger (fig. 127). While in the neighborhood don't miss the Oakland–San Francisco Bay Bridge designed by Timothy Pflueger, et al. Although built just a year before, it is not as elaborately detailed as the Golden Gate Bridge, but it still has its zigzags.

127. 99 Mission Street, former Rincon Annex Post Office.

11. 130 Montgomery Street.
Office building, designed by the O'Brien Brothers with Wilbur D. Peugh, and built in 1930.
It is a remarkable survivor with carved façade reliefs and window-spandrel trim intact.

12. 200 Montgomery Street.
Formerly the Bank of America, this building was remodeled by George Kelham in 1941.
The entrance lobby has an Art Deco version of classical coffering and splendid light fix-

128. 301 Pine Street, Pacific Stock Exchange; Earth's Fruitfulness sculpture by R. Stackpole.

tures. The Bank of America sailing-ship logo still remains on the elevator doors.

13. 343 Sansome Street.

This former Crown-Zellerback building was remodeled by Hyman and Appleton about 1930. It has been incorporated into the adjacent new highrise and in the process has suffered the loss of its lobby with marble walls, molded-plaster ceiling, and other detailing.

14. 301 Pine and 155 Sansome Street.

Pacific Coast Stock Exchange Building, built in 1915, and remodeled by Timothy Pflueger in 1929. The adjacent Stock Exchange Building was constructed at that time. Both buildings have art work by local artists, including the monumental sculptures flanking the portico entrance by Ralph Stackpole. The sculpture over the City Club entry is also by Stackpole.

The lobby is notable for the dark marble walls and gilded and faceted plaster ceiling. The City Club has a mural by Diego Rivera, the first of his murals to be done in this country. The City Club is a private club not open to the public (fig. 128).

15. 100 Bush Street.

Shell Building, designed by George Kelham, and built in 1928. The terra-cotta cladding has an unusual ripple finish, but the ornament is classic Deco with stylized floral and geometric forms. The exterior has a stepped profile with light pods located at the step back. The interior lobby has been remodeled and has lost some of its original elements. The ceiling was raised and a second floor opening and railing have been added. The upper office floors that contained original furnishings have been remodeled (see frontispiece, page ii; fig. 129).

129. 100 Bush Street, Shell Building; detail showing elevator doors. Photograph by Douglas Keister, Oakland, California.

San Francisco South of Market Street Walking Tour

The South of Market Area (SOMA) has always had an unusual look. When the area was first plotted by Jasper O'Farrell in the nineteenth century, he made no attempt to align the grid with the grid of streets north of Market Street. Much of the land was reclaimed from Mission Bay. The area has always had a mixed-use land pattern. Many of the buildings suffered in the 1906 disaster because of the soil conditions, but the area was rebuilt in much the same manner as it had existed before. The longer side of the blocks remained distinctly commercial or industrial in use, while the shorter side streets were residential. Many of the Deco buildings were architect designed.

1. 1355 Market Street.

Mart Building, formerly the Western Furniture Mart, designed by Capitol Architects, and built in 1937. The terra-cotta exterior has Mayan-inspired molded ornament. The recently refurbished lobby has restored light fixtures and a mural by Paul A. Schmitt.

2. 1500 Mission Street.

Commercial building, formerly White Motor Car Co., built in 1927, and remodeled by Henry Gutterson. The Streamline details include curved walls and stepped entry grillwork and tower (fig. 130).

3. 1517 Mission Street.

Commercial building, built in 1927; has a few decorative details remaining on the façade pilasters.

130. 1500 Mission Street, former White Motor Car Co. Building.

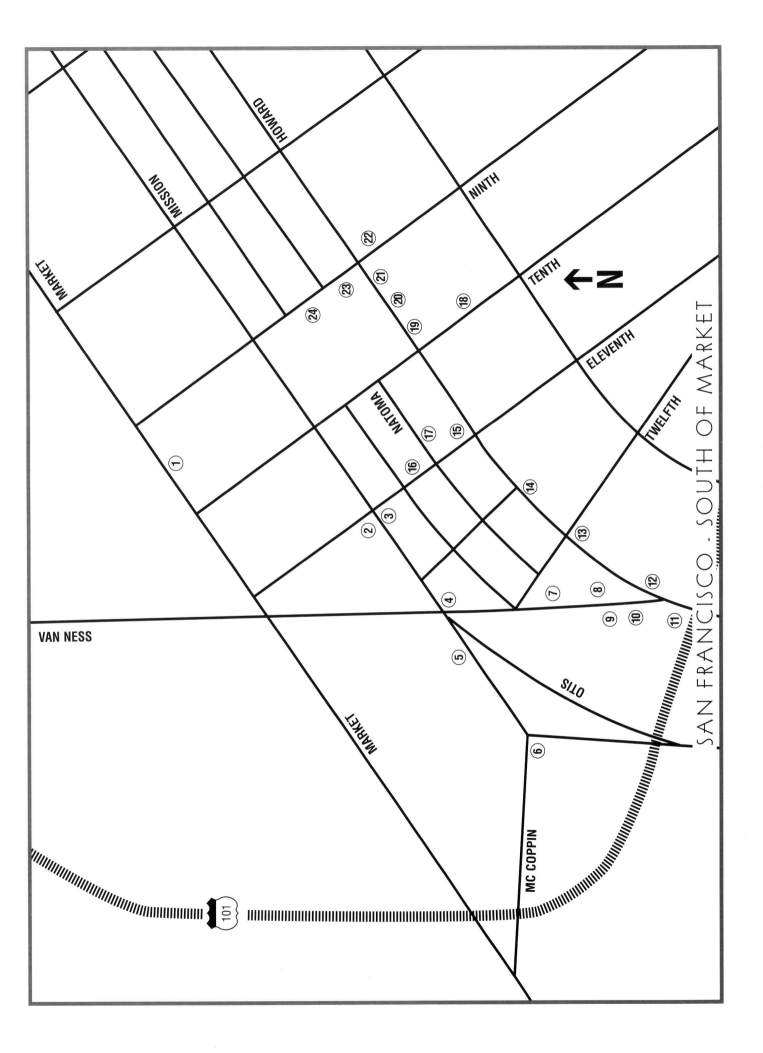

131. 1 McCoppin Street, Pacific Telephone Building.

4. 1581 Mission Street.

The former McCord Building was built in 1917 and remodeled in 1935 by Will P. Day. The Classic-style molded floral ornament was originally green.

5. 30 Otis Street.

Commercial building, built in 1931; has small-scale floral plaques at the top of the pilasters.

6. 1 McCoppin Street.

Pacific Telephone Company Building, designed by E.V. Cobby, and built in 1935. Cobby was a company architect and designed other exchange buildings in the city. The buff-color brick is enlivened with stylized floral terra-cotta window spandrels. The entry lobby has polychrome terrazzo (fig. 131).

7. 101 S. Van Ness Avenue.

Commercial building, built in 1935; has very simple detailing (fig. 132).

8. 123 S. Van Ness Avenue.

Industrial building, built in 1910, and remodeled about 1930–1935. The interior is graced with round-headed piers, ray motifs in the corners, and drop-pendant ornament.

9. 154 S. Van Ness Avenue.

Commercial building, built in 1938; has green and black Bakelite façade trim and glass blocks at the windows.

10. 160 S. Van Ness Avenue.

City and County of San Francisco Building, built in 1936. It reflects in its forms the trends in streamlining that had begun by this time.

132. 101 S. Van Ness Avenue, commercial building.

11. 170 S. Van Ness Avenue.
James H. Barry Co. Building, built in 1936; has a Mayan-arch doorway and floral panels inspired by Mayan motifs.

12. 1675 Howard Street.
Commercial building, formerly the Foremost Dairy Building, designed by Harry A. Thomasen, and built in 1937. It is a classic example of the Streamline style with

133. 969 Natoma Street, industrial building.

*134. 224 Townsend Street, indus-
trial building.*

*135. 255 10th Street, industrial
building.*

glass-block windows and a stepped tower. The glass-block windows on the first floor
were recently removed.

13. 210 12th Street.
Thomas Noble Co. Building, built in 1902 and Art Deco-ized about 1930–1935. The
changes included zigzags and new detailing at the corners of the building.

14. 1583 Howard Street.
Commercial building, built in 1932; has molded-plaster decoration in a chevron pattern, some of which is missing.

15. 1499 Howard Street.

Commercial building, built in 1939 in the Streamline style with a symmetrical façade and pulvinated speed lines over the entry canopy.

16. 165 11th Street.

Commercial building, built in 1931; has a black terra-cotta tile base, a porthole window in the entry door, and a circular light fixture.

17. 969 Natoma.

Utilitarian industrial building (fig. 133) built in 1906, and subsequently Art Deco-ized about 1935 taking its cue from 224 Townsend Street (fig. 134).

18. 255 10th Street.

Industrial building, built in 1932; has a stepped cornice and incised lines. Note the light pods flanking the entrance (fig. 135).

19. 1325-1331 Howard Street.

Commercial building, built in 1919, and Art Deco-ized about 1930–1935; has smooth stucco walls with black-glass inserts and rounded building corners.

20. 1309-1313 Howard Street.

Commercial building, built in 1915, and Art Deco-ized about 1930–1935; has unique squiggles on the façade.

21. 1251-1255-1261 Howard Street.

Industrial block built in 1936. The individual buildings are united behind an asymmetrical stucco façade with speed lines. Unfortunately, the other ornamentation was removed after the 1989 earthquake.

22. 190 9th Street.

Bowne Company Building, built in 1929, but somehow the Gothic detailing has a Deco touch.

23. 170-174 9th Street.

Industrial building, built in 1934; has stylized pilasters and wavy lines, a variant of zigzags.

24. 142 9th Street.

Industrial building, built in 1933; has molded-plaster zigzags.

San Francisco Upper Market Street Walking Tour

This is a short walking tour within just a few blocks of the University of California, Berkeley Extension campus, at Laguna and Market. The buildings are typical of the Art Deco buildings that can be found in every neighborhood of the city. They also show the spillover effect that a new building can have on an area. The Allen Arms Apartments apparently had just such an effect, causing other property owners to "modernize" their buildings.

1. 50 Laguna Street.
Apartment building, built in 1928. It has unusual decorative grilles at the entry door, transom, and sidelights. Although the original light fixtures remain, some of the ornamental plaster has been removed.

2. 16 Laguna Street.
Apartment building, built in 1931; distinguished by rays along the cornice line of the bays. The entry has decorative grilles in the door, transom, and sidelights, and notable plaster bas-reliefs.

3. 10-12-14 Laguna Street.
Although this flats building was built in 1931, the left side of the façade has a stepped parapet, while the right side retains a Mediterranean-style cartouche, so stylistically this is a split personality.

4. 4 Laguna Street.
Apartment building, built about 1910, definitely not Art Deco, but it shows what was old-fashioned by 1925. It has classically inspired ornament: a rinceau pattern with a face above the Ionic columns of the entry porch, egg-and-dart molding, brackets and dentils at the cornice level, enriched brackets with garlands between the bays, and wonderful stained glass with Art Nouveau designs.

5. 55 Hermann Street.
Allen Arms Apartments, designed by Herman C. Baumann, and built in 1928. This gore-shaped visual landmark is best viewed from Market Street, where it dominates the view coming up Market. It has a wealth of Art Deco detailing, including a stepped-arch entry, original light fixtures on the exterior and interior, "love bird" capitals on the pilasters, chevrons, rays, zigzags, etc. The undersides of the bays are decorated, a Baumann trait (see fig. 53). The lobby contains its original torchères, mirrors, and "Stock Exchange Building" molded-plaster ceiling.

6. 1890 Market Street.
Martens Market has a classic neon sign with speed lines and background box painting that are still intact. This additive sign was a typical way of giving a building a more modern look.

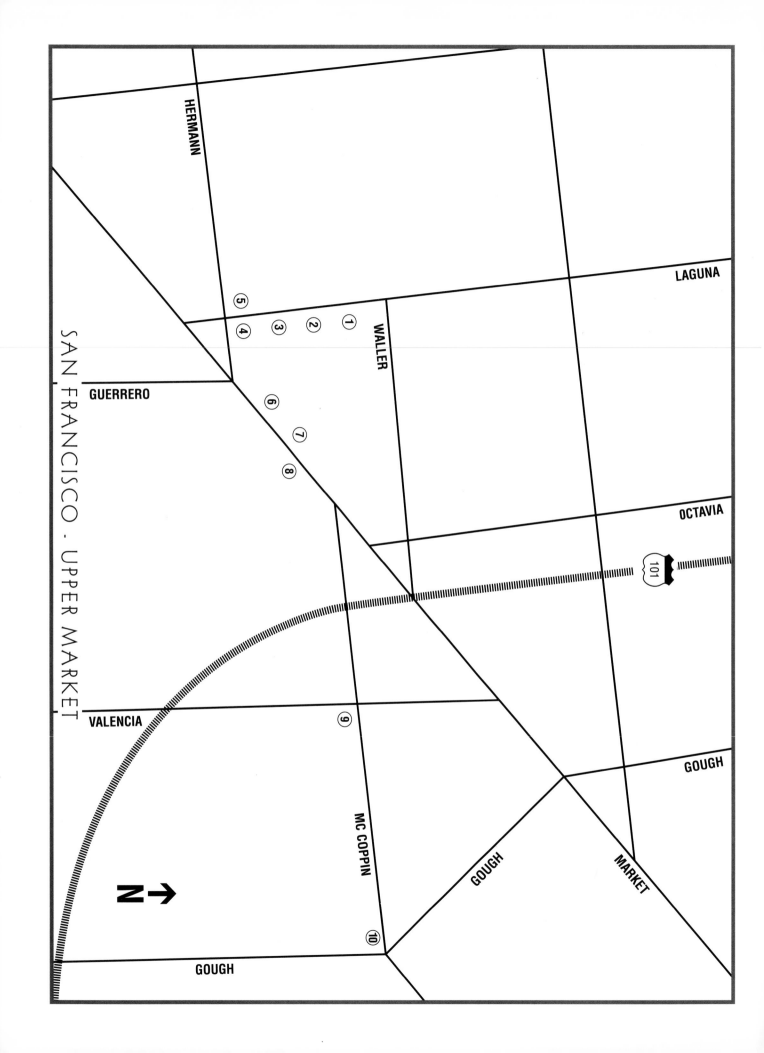

7. 1886 Market Street.

Built in 1932; has stucco prism-like projections and a zigzag cornice.

8. 1801 Market Street.

"Tops Fountain Coffee Shop" Building, built in 1907, and Art Deco-ized about 1930–1935. The notable vertical neon sign with speed lines and background box painting is intact. If you are interested in movies, don't miss the Limelight Film and Theater Bookstore at 1803 Market Street.

9. 170 Valencia Street.

Former fraternal-lodge building, built in 1931. The upper façade, best seen from the freeway above, still retains much of its original molded plaster ornament: stepped cornice, stylized floral patterns, and stepped entry arch.

10. 1 McCoppin Street.

Pacific Telephone Company Building, designed by E.V. Cobby, and built in 1935. Cobby was a company architect and designed other exchange buildings in the city. The buff-color brick is enlivened with stylized floral terra-cotta window spandrels. The entry lobby has polychrome terrazzo (see fig. 131).

Downtown Alameda Walking Tour

The Alameda walking tour is an opportunity to see the impact of Art Deco on a small town that could be located anywhere in the state. The "dressing up" of a Main Street, and here in Alameda it is Park Street, is typical of what occurred across the country from 1925 until the outbreak of World War II. Many of the designs found on these buildings are a distillation of more-elaborate motifs found on high-style buildings in the larger cities. The examples seen here often reveal the essential design elements of the style and the power they exercised when "modernization" was considered for a building.

1. 2317 Central Avenue.
Alameda Theater, designed by Timothy Pflueger, and built in 1931. It is an outstanding example of Deco theater style with a stepped façade, stylized floral bands, vertical neon sign, and a distinguished terrazzo entry. The flanking shopfronts have been altered, and the interior has suffered some losses, but it still remains a very strong presence in the neighborhood (figs. 136, 137).

2. 2320 Central Avenue.
Commercial building, built about 1925–1930; has Mayan-style transom windows and stepped pilasters (fig. 138).

3. 1364 Park Street.
Commercial building, built about 1935–1940. It has speed lines on the marquee, curved corners and window reveals, and both scalloped and wavy horizontal bands that show the influence of streamlining.

4. 1311-1305 Park Street.
Commercial building, built about 1930–1935; has stepped piers and maroon tile on the façade. The storefronts have been altered.

136. 2317 Central Avenue, Alameda Theater.

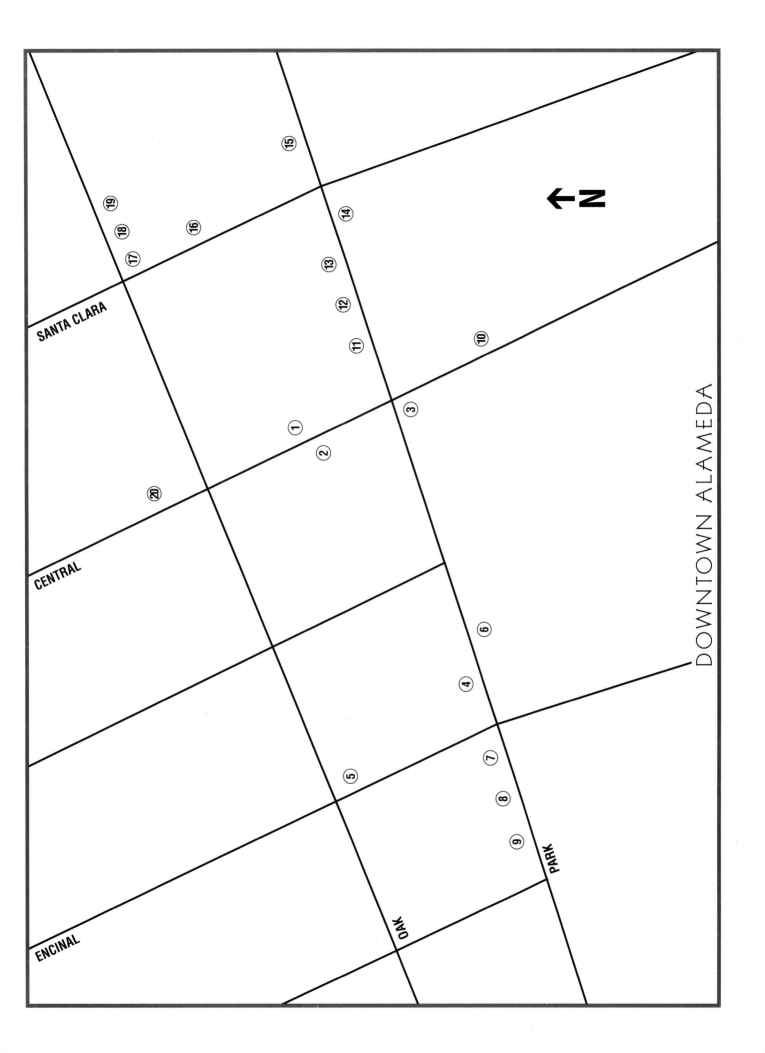

DOWNTOWN ALAMEDA

SANTA CLARA

CENTRAL

ENCINAL

OAK

PARK

*137. 2317 Central Avenue,
Alameda Theater; detail showing
floral decoration on façade.*

5. 2301 Encinal.

Former gas station, built about 1930–1935; has a stepped vertical sign, and speed lines on the marquee and on the building itself. The ancillary structure is similarly detailed. Typical of the gas stations that were erected by the major oil companies and often based on designs by such leading architects as Norman Bel Geddes.

6. 1222 Park Street.

Commercial building, built about 1935; has a stepped and curved façade that integrates the company sign, and a black-tile bulkhead.

*138. 2320 Central Avenue,
commercial building.*

7. 1215 Park Street.
Commercial building, built about 1935. It has a coating that obscures the tile work. The octagonal window suggests the mid-thirties construction date.

8. 1211 Park Street.
Commercial building, built about 1935, and still has the original color scheme of buff and brown terra-cotta tile work.

9. 1209-07 Park Street.
Commercial-residential building, built about 1935; has a scalloped cornice, tan and buff tiles, and speed lines between the windows.

10. 2423 Central Avenue.
Former grocery building, built about 1935–1940; has typical detailing from the period with pulvinated speed lines on the marquee, a tall vertical sign, and faceted yellow tile on the bulkhead.

11. 1407-13 Park Street.
Commercial building, built about 1935; has black and blue terra-cotta facing and original transom windows. The shopfront at 1411 has its original entry.

12. 1417 Park Street.
Boniere Bakery, dating about 1935, has black and buff Bakelite facing with glass-block windows, and a notable sign with original letters.

13. 1429-31 Park Street.
Commercial building, built about 1939; has a few remaining Art Deco details, such as the brise de soleil over the windows.

14. 1429-31 Park Street.
Commercial building, built in 1933; has octagonal floral medallions and vertical speed lines. The shopfronts have been altered.

15. 1507 Park Street.
Commercial building; has a notable neon sign for Ole's Waffle Shop, and also notice the Pop Inn sign further up the street.

16. 2305 Santa Clara.
Commercial building, built about 1940; has a green carrera-glass facing and a complementing green and yellow neon sign.

17. 2301 Oak Street.
Former Texaco Gas Station, built about 1935. It is typical of the designs used by the gasoline companies in that period. There may have been a tall vertical sign in neon.

18. 1510 Oak Street.
Knights of Pythias Building. It was Art Deco-ized about 1935 with smooth stucco and the addition of a stepped entry arch and stylized pilasters.

139. 2200 Central Avenue, Veterans Memorial Building.

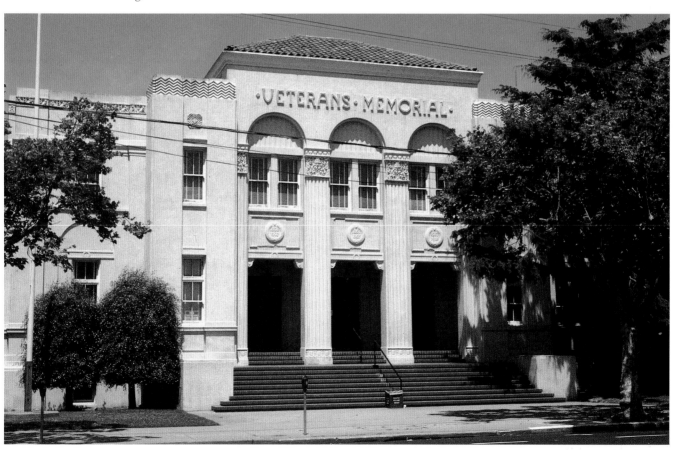

*140. 2200 Central Avenue,
Veterans Memorial Building;
detail of façade.*

19. 1516 Oak Street.
Times-Star Building, built in 1945, and is a late example of the style. The curved marquee, pulvinated speed lines, curved glass-block entry, and faceted window spandrels show the endurance of the design motifs.

20. 2200 Central Avenue.
Veterans Memorial Building, designed by Henry H. Meyers, a native of Alameda. It was built in 1929 with "Greco Deco" touches in the pilasters, zigzag cornice details, and stylized eagles over the doors. The interior is also notable because of the rich details that remain, including the color scheme in the auditorium with its original light fixtures (figs. 139, 140).

Downtown Berkeley Walking Tour

The Berkeley walking tour is centered around the public buildings in the vicinity of City Hall. Many of these buildings were designed by the well-known Berkeley architect James W. Plachek, in addition to the contribution of other notable local architects. It all adds up to a rich diversity of building types with handsome detailing.

1. 2274 Shattuck Avenue.
United Artists Theater, designed by C.A. Balch, and built in 1932. It has a "frozen fountain façade" (minus a tall vertical sign), and a lobby with decorative mirrors, light fixtures, and painted decorative motifs.

2. 2270 Shattuck Avenue.
Commercial building, built in 1905, but was remodeled in 1932 by the contractor F. J. Wallace. This remodeling job may have been in response to the new movie theater next door. The black and green terra-cotta tiles are a typical color scheme from the period.

3. 2909 Kittredge Street.
Berkeley Public Library, designed by James W. Plachek, and built in 1930. The exterior details are quite exotic, for there are ram's-head pilasters, and zigzags in the windows with cobra heads at the apex. The sgraffito decoration is by Simeon Pelenc.

4. 2000 Allston.
U.S. Post Office has WPA touches in the bas-relief by David Slivka to the left of the entrance, installed in 1937. There is a mural on the interior by Suzanne Scheuer from 1936. The depiction of historical themes in the mural is typical of the WPA mural art produced for public buildings.

5. Allston and Martin Luther King, Jr. Way.
Berkeley High School, designed by Henry Gutterson and Will Corlett, and built in 1939–1940. The large bas-reliefs on the walls are by Jacques Schier and Robert Boardman Howard, well-known local artists. The whole complex abounds in other wonderful details: curved entries, stylized buttresses, and elaborate bas-reliefs in the window spandrels. The long horizontal lines and curving elements give the unmistakable look of a Streamline building (fig. 141).

6. Allston, Martin Luther King, Jr. Way, and Center Street.
Civic Center Park, designed by Henry Gutterson, John Gregg, et al., and built in 1940. The fountain is not working, but it would have stepped cascades of water to complement the streamlined lines of the high school. There is a great view of the back of the City Hall.

7. 1931 Center Street.
Veterans Memorial Building, designed by Henry H. Meyers, and built in 1928. Here is another fine building in "Greco Deco" style, and with zigzags proliferating among the classical details (fig. 142).

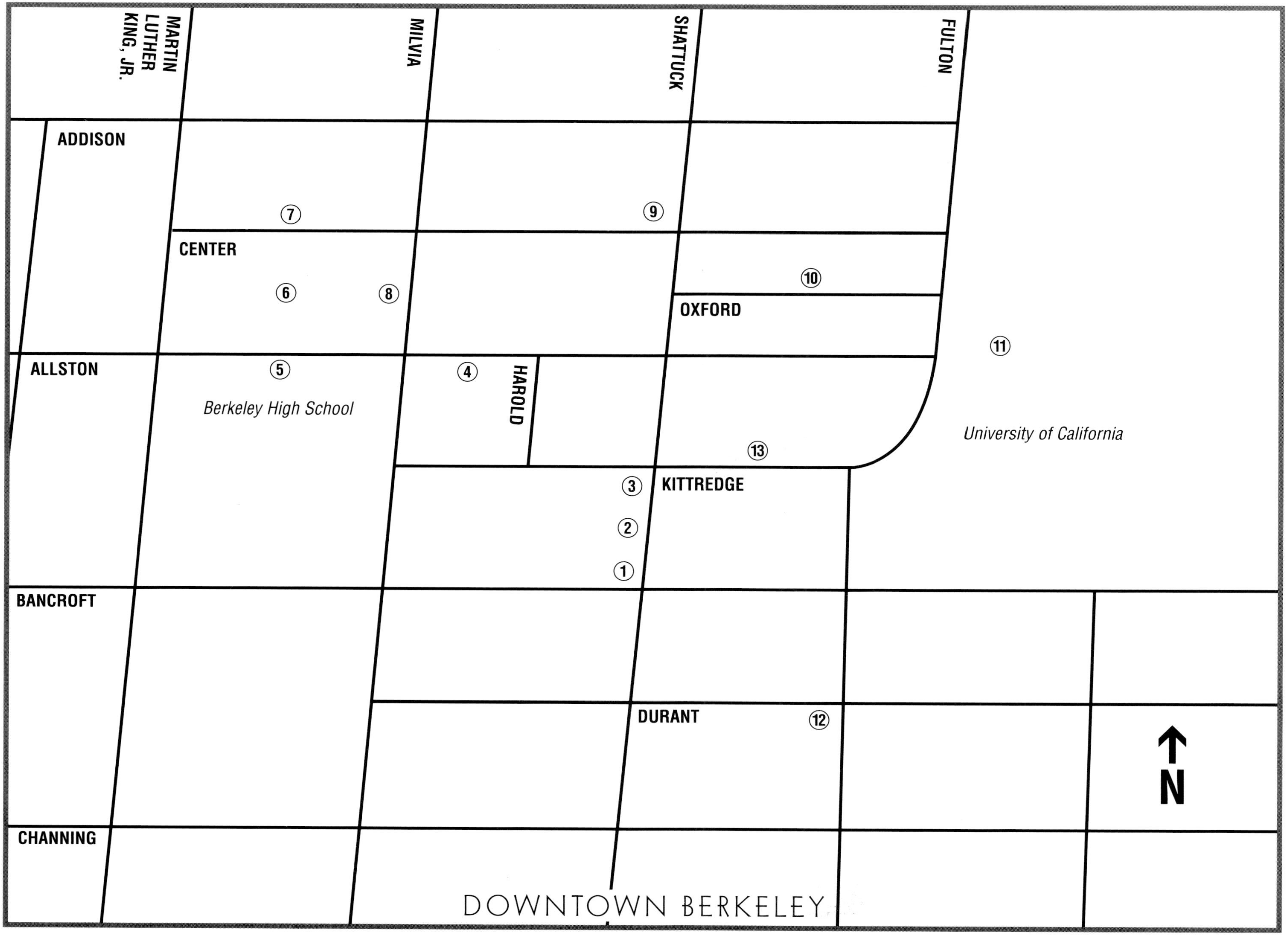

DOWNTOWN BERKELEY

N ←

University of California

Berkeley High School

FULTON

SHATTUCK

MILVIA

MARTIN LUTHER KING, JR.

ADDISON

CENTER

ALLSTON

OXFORD

HAROLD

KITTREDGE

BANCROFT

DURANT

CHANNING

① ② ③ ④ ⑤ ⑥ ⑦ ⑧ ⑨ ⑩ ⑪ ⑫ ⑬

141. Allston and Dr. Martin Luther King, Jr. Way, Berkeley High School.

142. 1931 Center Street, Veterans Memorial Building.

143. *2036 Shattuck Avenue, former Kress Department Store.*

8. 2180 Milvia Street.
Berkeley City Hall, formerly the Farm Credit Building, designed by James W. Plachek, and built in 1938. Its minimal detailing marks the trend toward streamlining.

144. *2036 Shattuck Avenue, former Kress Department Store;
detail showing fire escape.*

9. 2036 Shattuck Avenue.
Commercial building, former Kress Department Store, designed by company architect Edward Sibbert, and built in 1933. The buff-brick and terra-cotta trim are typical of the stores he designed for the company. The unusual designs of the terra cotta, the decorative fire escape, and poly-chrome terrazzo entries enliven the building (figs. 143, 144).

10. 2120 Oxford Street.
University of California Press Building, designed by Charles Masten and Lester Hurd, and built in 1931. The most notable feature is the long horizontal sweep of patterned glass-block windows.

11. University of California Campus.
Life Sciences Building, Men's Gymnasium, and Edwards Memorial Stadium (with Warren Perry) were designed by George Kelham. The Life Sciences Building is Kelham at his "Greco Deco" best; however, each one of these buildings has unusual detailing and it is well worth the walk through the campus to see them (fig. 145).

12. 2140 Durant.
Commercial building, designed by Frederick H. Reimers, and built in 1930. The patterned-brick exterior is enlivened with floral motifs.

145. University of California Campus; detail of Life Sciences Building.

146. 2111 Kittredge Street, California Theater.

13. 2111 Kittredge Street.
California Theater, built in 1911 and remodeled in 1929 by Balch and Stanbery; has a Buck Rogers-style marquee and neon sign in the blue and gold colors of the University of California (figs. 146, 147).

147. 2111 Kittredge Street, California Theater; detail of façade.

Uptown Oakland Walking Tour

The area of uptown Oakland developed after the City Hall moved to its present location on 14th Street about 1915. This move triggered additional changes that brought commercial development, including department stores, hotels, movie houses, and restaurants. The completion of the Key System rapid transit and the growth of the transportation node at Broadway and Grand completed the ascendancy of the area as the new downtown of Oakland. Unfortunately, some of the Art Deco buildings have not survived, and those remaining have an uncertain future. For guided-tour information call the Oakland Heritage Alliance at (510) 763-9218.

1. 1718 Telegraph Avenue and 1721 Broadway.
Commercial building, designed by Douglas Dacre Stone, and built in 1931. The terra-cotta façade on the south end of the building has been covered over, but the remaining terra cotta is notable for the black and silver pilasters incorporating light fixtures. The upper cornice has rays and stylized floral patterns with zigzags.

148. 1807-29 Telegraph Avenue, Oakland, Fox Theater and Building. Photograph by Douglas Keister, Oakland, California.

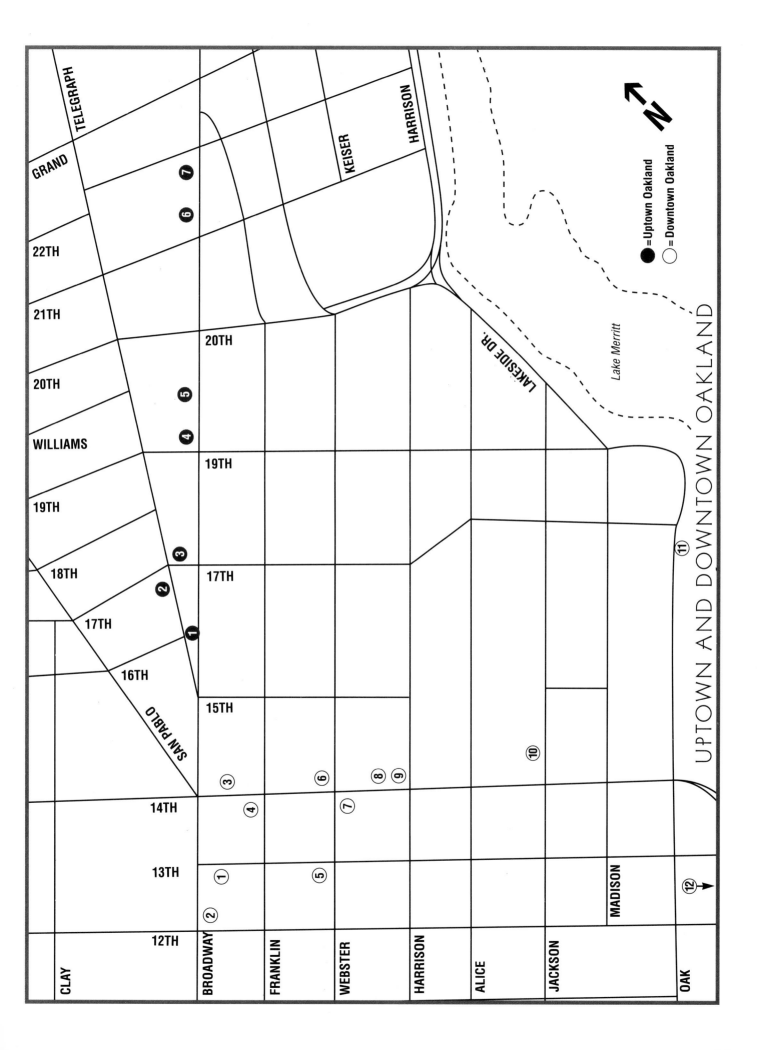

UPTOWN AND DOWNTOWN OAKLAND

149. 2001-11 Broadway,
I. Magnin Department Store.

150. 2025 Broadway, Paramount
Theater, Oakland; hall outside
auditorium. Photograph by
Douglas Keister, Oakland,
California.

2. 1807-29 Telegraph Avenue.

Fox Theater and Building, designed by
Weeks and Day (theater) and Maury I.
Diggs (office building), and built in 1928.
This exotic creation incorporating Hindu-
Islamic motifs has many notable features,
including terra-cotta tiles and forms. The
marquee and ticket booth were a 1935
addition designed by Alexander Aimwell
Cantin (fig. 148).

3. 1900-32 Telegraph Avenue.

Commercial building, designed by Albert
J. Evers, and built in 1931. An oustanding
example of polychrome terra cotta in
navy-blue and silver. The window frames
with zigzags abounding are aluminum (see
fig. 77).

4. 2001-11 Broadway.

I. Magnin & Co. Building, designed by Weeks and Day, and built in 1931. Here is
another outstanding example of colored terra cotta in one of the most popular colors
of the period—blue-green. The molded ornament includes zigzags and frozen fountains in the window spandrels (fig. 149). See also figure 75.

5. 2025 Broadway.

Paramount Theater, designed by Timothy Pflueger, and built in 1931. This is the

151. 2201 Broadway, former John Bruener Co. Building.

supreme example of Deco theater style in the Bay Area. The large "puppeteers" on the façade were inspired by one of the entrance gates at the 1925 Paris Exhibition. The spectacular interior has been restored to its original glory (fig. 150). It is open for tours the first and third Saturday of each month at 10 P.M. There is a nominal charge for the two-hour tour. See also figures 42, 43, and 44.

6. 2201 Broadway.

Commercial building, formerly the John Bruener Co., designed by Albert F. Roller, and built in 1931. The pale green terra-cotta exterior has molded, stylized floral details with light pods at the base of the second floor. The window spandrels have been altered (fig. 151). See also figure 76.

7. 2211-21 Broadway.

Clark-Jerner Building, designed by Reed and Corlett, and built in 1933. The terra-cotta tile has been painted, but the stepped details are still visible. There is also a notable neon sign that is still intact.

Downtown Oakland Walking Tour

This tour is located closer to the nineteenth-century center of Oakland in the area of Ninth and Broadway. Although the larger-scale buildings were erected slightly to the north, there are still a number of Art Deco buildings that vary in size and scale remaining in this area. Some are buildings constructed during the period and others a remodeling of earlier buildings. They all contribute to make this a fascinating look at Art Deco architecture. For guided-tour information call the Oakland Heritage Alliance at (510) 763-9218.

1. 427-449 13th Street.
Charles Jurgens Co. Building, designed by H.A. Minton, and built in 1935. The terra-cotta exterior is subtly faceted and has stylized floral designs and zigzag window lintels. The original exterior and interior light fixtures remain.

2. 1224 Broadway.
Commercial building, the former Lux Theater, has been drastically remodeled, but the aluminum panels flanking the entrance still remain as do some of the interior details. The neon marquee and vertical sign were removed at the command of the

152. 401 14th Street Financial Center Building, designed by Reed and Corlett, built in 1929; detail of entry. Photograph by Douglas Keister, Oakland, California.

City of Oakland.

3. 412-20 14th Street.

Elks Hall Building, originally built in 1903, and remodeled by Russell Guerne de Lappe in 1929. The green, buff, and black terra-cotta tile work is a typical color scheme of the period. There are stained-glass transoms with ray motifs hidden under a later covering.

4. 401 14th Street.

Financial Center Building, designed by Reed and Corlett, and built in 1929. Although some of the details are Gothic Revival in inspiration, the rest of the building contains innumerable Art Deco motifs, beginning with the stepped profile of the building. Unfortunately, the terra-cotta exterior has been sandblasted, but such details as stylized eagles remain in the spandrels. (Sandblasting is one of the most destructive treatments for any building.) The light fixtures in the lobby are original (figs. 152, 153).

5. 363-69 13th Street.

Central Building & Loan Association Building, designed by William E. Shirmer, and built in 1929. The splayed entry is surmounted by a bas-relief cornice panel containing classical figures with zigzag drapery.

6. 360-364 14th Street.

Commercial building, formerly the Bank of Oakland, designed by Frederick H. Reimers, and built in 1928. The faceted pilasters are topped with stylized eagle capitals. Other details include Mayan-arch transom windows, "winged" spandrels, and bas-relief panels by John Stoll.

7. 347 14th Street.

Anna Merriam Building, designed by C.W. McCall, and

153. 401 14th Street, Financial Center Building; detail showing floral decoration.

built in 1931. The color reflects the influence of the I. Magnin Store just a few blocks away. The jade-green terra cotta has pink highlights above a black terra-cotta bulkhead with zigzags.

8. 347 14th Street.
Ideal Cleaners has a notable façade with a neon sign and carrera-glass cladding. The planter boxes are a later addition.

9. 1413 Harrison Street.
Harrison Hotel received a touch of modernity about 1928 with the addition of the vertical neon sign attached to the corner of the building. It was a typical way of updating the look of a building.

10. 1431 Jackson Street.
Hill Castle Apartments, designed by Miller and Warnecke, and built in 1930. The rich details include stylized floral window spandrels with zigzags; stylized fountains; Mayan-arch entry doors and rooftop neon sign.

11. 1543-47 Lakeside Drive.
Scottish Rite Temple was originally built in 1927, but due to the deterioration of the

154. 1543-47 Lakeside Drive, Scottish Rite Temple.

stonework it was remodeled in 1939 by William G. Corlett with Deco touches. These include stylized Doric columns, a sunburst in the porch window, and figurative panels at the cornice (fig. 154).

12. 1225 Fallon Street.

Alameda County Courthouse, built in 1936, was a WPA project and designed by a committee of architects including William G. Corlett, H.A. Minton, James Plachek, and William E. Shirmer. The reinforced-concrete exterior is enlivened with terra-cotta trim on the stepped profile, faceted spandrels, fluted cornice, a stylized eagle above the entrance, and bronze entry surrounds with zigzags and rays. Eagles also decorate the lantern that crowns the courthouse. The interior has splendid marble mosaics designed by Marian Simpson that were added in 1938 (figs. 155, 156).

155. 1225 Fallon Street, Alameda County Courthouse.

156. 1225 Fallon Street,
Alameda County Courthouse;
detail showing entrance.

157. Golden Gate Bridge; Joseph
Strauss was the engineer, and
Irving Morrow the architect; com-
pleted in 1937.

GLOSSARY

The terms listed below are intended to be a guide to the comments contained in the text. Many of the terms are derived from standard architectural terms; however, Art Deco architects often played fast and loose with forms so that some latitude has been given especially in the interpretation of traditional terms.

Brace-shaped. The shape of molded terra-cotta tile that in profile is a rounded section flanked by points.

Brise-soleil. A narrow ledge-like construction that is located above a door or a window to act as a sunblock. Often the corners are rounded, and sometimes they have pulvinated lines.

Canted. Having a slant.

Clathri. A web-like look given to a window by glazing bars in an X shape combined with a + shape.

Cornice. The top or finishing molding that occurs at the roofline on the exterior of a building, or at the ceiling level in an interior.

Frieze. The continuous decorative band along a wall that is often found at the base of bays, and continuing along the full width of the façade.

Glass inserts. Glass block, or sometimes black or colored structural glass which is referred to as carrera glass or by various trade names such as Vitrolux, and which is found in wall surfaces.

Incised. Cut into the surface.

Lights. The opening between the mullions of a window that is glazed. Also used to describe glazed openings in doors.

Mayan arch. An arch having a slanted rise, and which sometimes has a truncated apex, is sometimes stepped, or has two different pitches. Such an arch is often found at the top of a bay in apartments or residences.

Molded. Raised from the surrounding surface and having a two-dimensional surface.

Molding. A raised continuous strip of decoration, usually found at the base of bays, at ceiling level, or at cornice level.

Muntins. The glazing bars in a window.

Parapet. The section of a wall that rises above the roof level behind it.

Pier. A masonry support, which is different from a column, and does not have the usual base, shaft, and capital. Sometimes it has a stepped profile, a prism profile, or a stepped head.

Plaques. Raised, molded ornament, often found in a circular shape as in a roundel or in an octagonal shape.

Porthole window. A small circular window. Sometimes it will have wheel-like muntins, or it may be faced over with speed lines, such as three strips of metal.

Prism. A raised form with a triangular profile that often terminates in a pointed shape at the ends. If the ends of a group of prisms are set in a touching sequence, they can form a zigzag in plan or profile.

Pulvinated. Raised from the surrounding surface with a convex shape.

Raised. Having a sharp edge that separates the object from the surrounding surface. Usually used for speed lines or ornamental plaques.

Reeding. Decoration of parallel convex moldings touching one another, often found at the cornice of bays.

Reveal. The part of the jamb that lies between the window glass or door and the outer wall surface. If it is cut diagonally, it is called splayed.

Scallop. An ornament carved or molded in the form of a shell or having a continuous pattern of half-round forms.

Sgraffito. Decoration on a plastered or stuccoed surface, with the top coat cut through to show a differently colored surface below.

Sidelights. The large windows, usually inoperable, that flank an entry door. They can be clear-glazed, frosted glass, or glass-block, often with decorative grilles.

Spandrel. The space between the head of one window and the sill of the window above. This space usually contains some kind of ornamentation on Art Deco buildings.

Splay. A sloping, chamfered surface cut into a wall, usually around doors or windows.

Speed lines. Parallel lines that can be raised, pulvinated, or incised. They usually occur in groups of three, but sometimes there is only a single line. Speed lines can be both horizontal or vertical.

Terra-cotta. A building material used as both a facing material and as a veneer, depending on the depth and size of the unit.

Transom. The bar above a door or window that separates it from a glazed opening. The term is sometimes used to refer to the window itself. A transom can be clear-glazed or glass-block, and will often have decorative grilles.

Tympanum. The area of the space between the lintel of a doorway and the arch above.

ART DECO SOCIETIES

Baton Rouge
ART DECO SOCIETY OF LOUISIANA
PO Box 1326, Baton Rouge LA 70821-1320
(504) 275-6367

Boston
ART DECO SOCIETY OF BOSTON
1 Murdock Terrace, Brighton MA 02135
(617) 787-2637 FAX (617) 782-4430

Charleston
ART DECO SOCIETY OF SOUTH CAROLINA—
Charleston Chapter
856-A Liriope Lane, Mt. Pleasant SC 29464
(803) 849-9289

Chicago
CHICAGO ART DECO SOCIETY
400 Skokie Boulevard, Suite #270, Northbrook IL
60062 (708) 291-4440

Cleveland
ART DECO SOCIETY OF NORTHERN OHIO
3439 West Brainard Road, #260, Woodmere OH
44122 (216) 831-9110

Cleveland
ART DECO SOCIETY OF CLEVELAND
3300 Green Road, Beachwood OH 44122
(216) 621-5255

Detroit
DETROIT AREA ART DECO SOCIETY
PO Box 1393, Royal Oak MI 48068-1893
(313) 886-3443

Los Angeles
ART DECO SOCIETY OF LOS ANGELES
PO Box 972, Hollywood CA 90078 (213) 639-DECO

Miami
MIAMI DESIGN PRESERVATION LEAGUE
PO Bin L, Miami Beach FL 33119 (305) 672-2014
FAX (305) 672-3419

New York
ART DECO SOCIETY OF NEW YORK
385 5th Avenue, Suite #501, New York NY 10016
(212) 679-DECO

Palm Beaches
ART DECO SOCIETY OF THE PALM BEACHES
820 Lavers Circle #G 203, Delray Beach FL 33444
(407) 276-9925

Sacramento
SACRAMENTO ART DECO SOCIETY
PO Box 162836, Sacramento CA 95816-2836
(916) 391-3964

San Francisco
ART DECO SOCIETY OF CALIFORNIA
100 Bush Street, #511, San Francisco CA 94104
(415) 982-DECO

Washington, D.C.
ART DECO SOCIETY OF WASHINGTON
PO Box 11090, Washington, D.C. 20008
(202) 298-1100

Melbourne, Australia
SOCIETY ART DECO VICTORIA
PO Box 1324, Collingwood, Victoria, Australia, 3066
(61) 03-419-8741

Perth, Australia
ART DECO SOCIETY OF WESTERN AUSTRALIA
182 Broome Street, Cottesloe, 6011, West Australia

Sydney, Australia
ART DECO SOCIETY OF NEW SOUTH WALES
PO Box 752, Willoughby, N.S.W., 2068, Australia
(61) 02-419-4259

Canada
CANADIAN ART DECO SOCIETY
101-1080 Barclay Street, Vancouver, BC V6E 1G7,
Canada (604) 662-7623

England
THE TWENTIETH CENTURY SOCIETY (formerly
"The Thirties Society")
58 Crescent Lane, London, SW4 9PU, England
(071) 738-8480

New Zealand
ART DECO TRUST, INC.
PO Box 133, Napier, New Zealand (64) 06-835-0022
FAX (64) 06-835-3984

SUGGESTIONS FOR FURTHER READING

Albrecht, Donald, *Designing Dreams, Modern Architecture in the Movies*. New York: Harper & Row, 1986. It was during the Art Deco period that the movies served to bring the concepts of modern design and architecture to the movie-going public. This book shows how that occurred, who the designers were, which stars were involved, and the impact that this had on design in America. Copious black-and-white illustrations of movie stills and sets enliven the text. Bibliography.

Arwas, Victor, *Art Deco*. New York: Harry N. Abrams, Inc., 1980. This is the standard large-scale text covering the entire range of Art Deco, with the exception of architecture. There is very good coverage of the 1925 Paris Exposition with period photographs. The sections cover interiors, furniture, silver, jewelry, bookbinding. Color plates and black-and-white illustrations. Bibliography.

Baker, Eric and Blik, Tyler, *Trademarks of the 20's and 30's*. San Francisco: Chronicle Books, 1985. Advertising began to reach new heights during the Deco period, and the importance of a modern image projected to the viewing public became of great importance. This book presents these images in a booklet format. Black-and-white illustrations.

Baker, Patricia, *Art Deco Source Book*. Secaucus, New Jersey: Wellfleet Press, 1988.

Battersby, Martin, *Art Deco Fashion, French Designers 1908–1925*. New York: St. Martin's Press, 1974.

——, *The Decorative Thirties*, revised and edited by Philippe Garner. New York: Whitney Library of Design, 1988.

——, *The Decorative Twenties*, revised and edited by Philippe Garner. New York: Whitney Library of Design, 1988.

Brunhammer, Yvonne, *The Nineteen Twenties Style*. New York: The Hamlyn Publishing Group Limited, 1969.

——, *Art Deco Style*. New York: St. Martin's Press, 1984.

Camard, Florence, *Ruhlmann, Master of Art Deco*. New York: Harry N. Abrams, Inc., 1984. Initially in the 1930s, American furniture of the period was heavily influenced by designs emanating from Europe. This text documents the career of one of the premier French designers who had an influence on American design. His oeuvre includes not only furniture but also textiles, light fixtures, and interiors. His influence in America is not discussed. Color plates, black-and-white photographs. Bibliography.

Capitman, Barbara, *Deco Delights: Preserving the Beauty and Joy of Miami Beach Architecture*. New York: E. P. Dutton, 1988. The author devoted the latter part of her life to saving Miami Beach's embattled Art Deco buildings and to establish the Art Deco Historical District. This book, which is lavishly illustrated with many color plates, shows the reason for this fervor.

——, Michael D. Kinerk, and Dennis W. Wilhelm, *Rediscovering Art Deco U.S.A.* New York: Viking Studio Books, 1994. This is a comprehensive study of significant examples of Art Deco architecture in twenty cities throughout the U.S.A. Color plates and black-and-white photographs.

Carpenter, Patricia F. and Totah, Paul, editors, *The San Francisco Fair Treasure Island 1939–1940*. San Francisco: Scotwall Associates, 1989. The book comprises reminiscences of the people who worked at or visited the World's Fair held on the man-made Treasure Island in San Francisco Bay. The stories provide insight into the feelings of the period, and the many contemporary black-and-white and color illustrations provide important visual information about current styles and what was to come in architectural design in the San Francisco Bay Area.

Cerwinske, Laura, *Tropical Deco: The Architecture and Design of Old Miami Beach*. New York: Rizzoli International Publications, Inc., 1981. Art Deco had many style variations, but Miami Beach has one of the largest concentrations of the style that truly reflects local sources in materials and design elements. These include the use of local tinted coral stone and a variety of nautical themes as decorative elements. Color photographs.

The Cunard White Star Quadruple-Screw Liner Queen Mary, reprint of advertisements. New York: Bonanza Books, 1979. During the Deco period, ocean travel reached new heights in speed and elegance. This book reproduces some of the original advertising that promoted the *Queen Mary*, which had been designed to compete with the French Line's *Normandie* and *Ile de*

France. Many black-and-white photographs of the liner's interiors and the mechanical systems provide great period photodocumentation. The *Queen Mary* is now berthed permanently in Long Beach, California, and is open for visits.

Delhaye, Jean, *Art Deco Posters and Graphics*. London: Academy Editions, and New York: St. Martin's Press, 1977.

DeNoon, Christopher, *Posters of the WPA*. Los Angeles: The Wheatley Press, 1987. The WPA Arts Projects included divisions for easel painting, sculpture, and graphics. Although few graphic works have survived, this publication documents not only the development of the graphics division but also the designers involved, the subject matter, and the influence of European design. Many of the designers went into private industry when the project ended, but it was not until after World War II that American advertising began to show the influence of these designers. Color plates, black-and-white photographs. Bibliography.

Doordan, Dennis P., *Architecture in Context: The Modern Movement*, Aspects of Architectural Drawings in the Modern Era. Chicago: The Art Institute of Chicago, 1988. This short exhibition catalog contains several important illustrations that show the development of design in America during the period. Drawings and black-and-white photographs. Bibliography.

Duncan, Alastair, *American Art Deco*. New York: Harry N. Abrams, Inc., 1986.

——, *Art Deco Furniture*. New York: Holt, Rinehart and Winston, 1984. Color plates. This encyclopedia of period furniture is lavishly illustrated in color with the premier examples of the work of the premier designers of the period. Included is an alphabetical listing of designers with brief biographies. Bibliography.

——, *Art Nouveau and Art Deco Lighting*. London: Thames and Hudson, 1978.

——, ed. *The Encyclopedia of Art Deco*. New York: E.P. Dutton, 1988.

Fry, Charles Rahn, *Benedictus' Art Deco Designs in Color*. New York: Dover Publications, Inc., 1980. Edouard Benedictus was a leading French designer during the period. This book reproduces the folios that he produced with the intention of providing copyrighted source material for other designers. The designs and their unusual colors show the influence of Cubism. Fauvism, and other art movements of the period. Color plates.

——, editor, *Art Deco Designs in Color*. New York: Dover Publications, Inc., 1975. This book includes the designs of many artists and designers of the period, including Sonja Delaunay, E.-A. Seguy, and others. Color plates.

——, editor, *Art Deco Interiors in Color*. New York: Dover Publications, Inc., 1977.

Fusco, Tony, *The Official Identification and Price Guide to Art Deco*. New York: House of Collectibles, 1988.

Gaston, Mary Frank, *Collector's Guide to Art Deco*. Paducah, Kentucky: Collector's Books, 1989.

Gebhard, David and Von Breton, Harriette, *Los Angeles in the Thirties, 1931–1941*. Layton, Utah: Peregrine Smith, 1975.

Goldberger, Paul, *The Skyscraper*. New York: Alfred A. Knopf, Inc., 1981. This book discusses the development of the skyscraper, epitomized by the Chrysler Building, Empire State Building, and Rockefeller Center. Color and black-and-white photographs. Bibliography.

Griffin, Leonard, Louis K. Meisel, Susan Pear Meisel, *Clarice Cliff: The Bizarre Affair*. New York: Harry N. Abrams, Inc., 1988. Clarice Cliff was one of the premier English pottery designers of the 1920s and 1930s, and her brilliantly colored teaware and dinnerware are typical of the period at its jazzy best. Color plates, black-and-white photographs.

Hall, Carolyn, *The Twenties in Vogue*. New York: Harmony Books, 1983.

Hanks, David A. and Jennifer Toher, *Donald Deskey; Decorative Designs and Interiors*. New York: E.P. Dutton, 1987. Donald Deskey was trained in both the United States and Europe. This book documents his remarkable career in all phases of modern design. Deskey is best known for his magnificent decorative designs for New York's Radio City Music Hall. Color plates and black-and-white photographs. Bibliography.

Hillier, Bevis, *Art Deco*. New York: E. P. Dutton, 1968. This small "Pictureback" was the first book on the subject to be published after World War II. Color plates and black-and-white photographs.

_____, *The Style of the Century 1900–1980*. New York: E. P. Dutton, Inc., 1983.

_____, *The World of Art Deco*. New York: E. P. Dutton, Inc., 1971. This is the catalog of the monumental exhibition of over 1400 objects held at The Minneapolis Institute of Arts, July 8 - September 5, 1971. Color plates and black-and-white photographs.

Ingle, Marjorie, *The Mayan Revival Style: Art Deco Mayan Fantasy*. Salt Lake City: Gibbs M. Smith, Inc., Peregrine Smith Books, 1984. This book is the result of graduate work and reflects a thorough knowledge of the origins of the revival of the style during the late 1920s and early 1930s. Variants can be found throughout the country, although many of the full-blown examples are located in Southern California. Color plates and black-and-white photographs. Bibliography.

Ives, Heather, *The Art Deco Architecture of Napier*. Napier, New Zealand: Ministry of Works and Development, 1982. Napier and its sister city, Hamilton, were destroyed by an earthquake in 1931. During the reconstruction, the citizens chose an amalgamation of "Hollywood–Santa Barbara Style," that combines the red-tile roofs of Santa Barbara and the Art Deco ornament of Hollywood to create an international style with touches of local Maori designs. The illustrations include many period photographs of both exteriors and interiors. Also provided are biographies of the principal architects involved. Black-and-white photographs. Bibliography.

Kery, Patricia Frantz, *Art Deco Graphics*. New York: Harry N. Abrams, Inc., 1986. Advertising and graphics took on a very different look in the 1920s and 1930s. This book documents the influences from contemporary art movements, the artists involved, and the international scope of the changes in design. Also included are wallpaper, book jacket, and packaging designs. Color plates and black-and-white photographs. Bibliography.

Klein, Dan, Nancy A. McClelland, and Malcolm Haslam, *In the Deco Style*. New York: Rizzoli International Publications, Inc., 1986.

_____, *All Color Book of Art Deco*. London: Octopus Books Limited, 1974.

Lesieutre, Alain, *The Spirit and Splendour of Art Deco*. Secaucus, New Jersey: Castle Books, 1974.

Loewy, Raymond, *Industrial Design*. Woodstock, New York: The Overlook Press, 1979.

Madigan, Mary Jean, *Steuben Glass: An American Tradition in Crystal*. New York: Harry N. Abrams, Inc., 1982. While this book documents the entire development of Steuben Glass through the 1980s, it contains important sections on design developments during the 1920s and 1930s. Color plates and black-and-white photographs. Bibliography.

Mandelbaum, Howard and Eric Myers, *Screen Deco: A Celebration of High Style in Hollywood*. New York: St. Martin's Press, 1985. This book shows how modern ideas in design, furniture, and interiors were incorporated in the movies. Many black-and-white illustrations of movie stills and sets. Bibliography.

Marling, Karal Ann, *Wall-to-Wall America: A Cultural History of the Post-Office Murals in the Great Depression*. Minneapolis: University of Minnesota Press, 1982.

McClinton, Katherine Morrison, *Art Deco, A Guide for Collectors*. New York: Clarkson N. Potter, Inc., Publishers, 1972.

Miller, Samuel C., *Neon Techniques & Handling* (reprint). Cincinnati: Signs of the Times Publishing Co., 1977. Originally published in the 1930s, this book is still the standard manual for neon design and sign bending, first introduced in America in 1925. It includes a brief discussion of the development of the medium and details the technological aspects of the craft. Drawings.

Mouron, Henri, *A.M. Cassandre*. New York: Rizzoli International Publications, Inc., 1985. Henri Mouron is the son of Adolphe Mouron, known as A. M. Cassandre. This book documents the career of one of the premier graphic artists of the period. Cassandre's career began before the 1925 Paris Exposition, where he won a gold prize for his poster designs, and continued into the 1960s with his design for the Yves St. Laurent logo. His later work encompassed not only posters and graphics but also theater sets, costume designs, and portraiture. Color plates and black-and-white photographs. Bibliography.

Raulet, Sylvie, *Art Deco Jewelry*. New York: Rizzoli International Publications, Inc. 1984. This book documents the work of the outstanding jewelry designers during the Deco period. Color plates and black-and-white photographs. Bibliography.

Robinson, Cervin and Rosemarie Haag Bletter, *Skyscraper Style: Art Deco New York*. New York: Oxford University Press, 1975.

Robinson, Julian, *The Brilliance of Art Deco*. New York/London: Bartley & Jensen, Publishers, 1989.

——, *The Golden Age of Style, Art Deco Fashion Illustration*. New York: Gallery Books, 1976.

——, *Fashions in the '30s*. London: Universal Books Limited, 1978.

Root, Keith, *Miami Beach Art Deco Guide*. Miami Beach, Florida: Miami Design Preservation League, 1987.

Scarlett, Frank and Marjorie Townley, *Arts Décoratifs 1925: A Personal Recollection of the Paris Exhibition*. London: Academy Editions and New York: St. Martin's Press, 1975. This book is a reminiscence of two of the artists who participated in the construction and exhibition of the English pavilion at the 1925 Paris Exposition. Numerous black-and-white photographs illustrate the other exhibitions and pavilions at the exposition.

Seguy, E.-A., *Exotic Floral Patterns in Color*. New York: Dover Publications, Inc., 1974.

Sembach, Klaus-Jurgen, *Style 1930*. New York: Universe Books, 1986.

Shaw, Peter and Peter Hallett, *Art Deco Napier: Styles of the Thirties*. Auckland, New Zealand: Reed Methuen Publishers, Inc., 1987. Art Deco may have developed in Europe, but its influence on design was worldwide. This book chronicles the rebuilding of Napier and its sister city of Hamilton that were destroyed by an earthquake in 1931 and rebuilt in the "Hollywood–Santa Barbara Style." It also documents the influence of Maori design on decorative elements.

Stern, Rudi, *Let There Be Neon*. New York: Harry N. Abrams, Inc., 1979.

Stone, Susannah Harris, *The Oakland Paramount*. Berkeley, California: Lancaster-Miller Publishers, 1981. This superbly illustrated book documents the remarkable National Historic Landmark theater in Oakland, California. The theater is one of the crown jewels in the distinguished career of San Francisco architect Timothy Pfleuger. Also included are many contemporary photographs by Gabriel Moulin. Color plates and black-and-white photographs. Bibliography.

Van de Lemme, Arie, *A Guide to Art Deco*. Secaucus, New Jersey: Chartwell Books, Inc., 1986.

Weber, Eva, *Art Deco in America*. New York: Exeter Books, 1985.

Whiffen, Marcus and Carla Breeze, *Pueblo Deco, The Art Deco Architecture of the Southwest*. Albuquerque, New Mexico: University of New Mexico Press, 1984. In this book noted architectural historian Marcus Whiffen discusses the influence of American Indian design on a variety of buildings in the American Southwest. Color plates and architectural drawings. Bibliography.

Wilson, Richard Guy, Dianne H. Pilgrim, and Dickran Tashjian, *The Machine Age in America, 1918–1941*. New York: Harry N. Abrams, Inc., 1986. This is the catalog for an exhibition originating at The Brooklyn Museum, Brooklyn, New York. The show covered all aspects of design from toasters to bridges to show the influence of the machine and the machine-look on design. Early influences, new materials, designers, and exhibitions are all discussed in well-written essays. Color plates and black-and-white photographs. Bibliography.